# DIVINE LOGISTICS

*Divine Logistics:*
A real world guide to getting past the titles and onto the work of executing exemplary ministry.

Copyright © 2011 by Vicky R. Johnson

All rights reserved

Published by *holy matrimony* Baltimore, Maryland
www.divinelogistics.org

Permission to reproduce or transmit in any form or by any means, electronic or mechanical, including photocopying and recording, or by any information storage and retrieval system, must be obtained in writing from the author, Vicky R. Johnson

Scripture quotations taken from the Amplified® Bible,
Copyright © 1954, 1958, 1962, 1964, 1965, 1987 by The Lockman Foundation
Used by permission." (www.Lockman.org)

THE HOLY BIBLE, NEW INTERNATIONAL VERSION®, NIV® Copyright © 1973, 1978, 1984, 2010 by Biblica, Inc.™ Used by permission. All rights reserved worldwide.

Scripture taken from *The Message*. Copyright � 1993, 1994, 1995, 1996, 2000, 2001, 2002. Used by permission of NavPress Publishing Group.

To order additional copies of this title, contact your local bookstore or call 202-517-9189

For speaking engagements, book signings and course instruction the author may be contacted at the following address:
Post Office Box 9476
Catonsville, Maryland 21228
Phone 202-517-9189
Email info@divinelogistics.org

Websites www.divinelogistics.org www.eprealitycheck.com
www. holymatrimonyonline.com, www.eventsbyhm.com

Cover Design and Illustration by Justin C. Henry
Page design by Vicky Johnson
Printed by Createspace
Library of Congress Cataloging in Publication Data
2011903978

ISBN: 978-0615461083

# TABLE OF CONTENTS

| | |
|---|---|
| FOREWORD | 5 |
| EVENTS AS MINISTRY | 9 |
| NEW TESTAMENT MINISTRY | 15 |
| A.C.T.S.†ASCERTAIN | 19 |
| A.C.T.S.†CALCULATE | 31 |
| A.C.T.S.†TAILOR | 37 |
| A.C.T.S.†STEERING | 43 |
| TAKE IT TO CHURCH | 49 |
| THAT VOLUNTEER SPIRIT | 71 |
| CREATING THE STANDARD | 79 |
| EXPANDING YOUR REACH | 99 |
| THE PUBLIC EYE | 105 |
| DOWN THE AISLE | 111 |
| WEDDINGS ON YOUR OWN | 121 |
| BUILDING YOUR TEAM | 145 |
| CREATING THE EXPERIENCE | 161 |
| EPILOGUE | 171 |
| GLOSSARY | 173 |

# FOREWORD

The field of event planning has become widely popular, even glamorous. As the world has been afforded a closer look "back stage" at the inner workings of this industry, the industry as a whole and its professionals have moved to the forefront of popularity and are showcased for the brilliance of the delivery of their craft.

The push for more glitz and glamour to be showered on events as well as the demand, by the client, for bigger, better, bolder events draws more and more individuals into the fold, wanting to be a part of the action.

This is great for the industry. But with every good thing there is always a drawback. Very often I witness the lack of "authentic" creativity and design as well as the inability or unwillingness of individuals to identify and compensate those persons with a specifically sought after talent under the guise "I can do this myself equally as well for less." I also witness the lack of honest to goodness hard work that every single one of these events demands. These factors have created a glut of what I term, industry "participants".

Event planning is more than decorating; it's more than an attention to detail and being organized.  This industry demands all of that and more. It's about always firing on all cylinders; it's the understanding that the event is only as strong as the weakest vendor, the weakest team member, the dropped ball, the lame excuse.

This industry is about the expectation of excellence, no matter the budget, the number of attendees or the identity of the guest of honor. It is plans and back up plans, it is pulling rabbits out of hats and always having yet one more option available in case of disaster. It is out of pocket expenses that do not get reimbursed. It is working for the client and not the camera. It is surrounding yourself with strong and committed players whom you value and who respect you. They are committed to putting in the work because they TRUST that you are committed to putting in the work.

It is for all of these reasons I choose to speak to ministry. I serve in an array of capacities within a ministry that executes to a high standard and yet I still see gaps that, in my eyes, often appear simple to fix. I too acknowledge that the church, and the congregations it serves, requires more than a quick fix to update and alter the behaviors and techniques that have been in place for ages and are the cornerstone for the ministry as it stands today.

It's evident the mainstream industry is tightening itself up, yet it seems that many faith based organizations are lagging behind in the higher implementation of these same techniques as it pertains to how things are run. Far too many churches are operating from a standpoint of *"the way we've always done it..."*, but its objectives are ever growing. We need to keep in stride with technology, volunteer training, and excellence in execution to grow, reach and serve a savvy community that can always benefit from another opportunity to **Meet Christ**.

*I have searched all over*, scouring the bookshelves, but could find no one that was speaking directly to the logistical operation of our church's services and events. A guide for creating better and more effective events. One that explains how its implementation and execution could provide growth opportunities and more importantly make ministry more accessible to those in need. I believe that if we get it right here, we can take it to levels not yet realized. Every wedding, funeral, women's conference, youth fest, revival, and visiting musical artist should blow folks out of the water if your ministry is behind the scenes. Get it right here and where you take it from there is limited only by the vision already planted within you.

# CERTIFICATION
### *What is the value of a certification both internally and externally?*

The event planning industry is a field that does not require one specific certification or licensure enabling you to operate.

However certification  attests to the fact that you have been trained, assessed and verified by an industry recognized professional or educational institute that upholds industry practices and standards of operation.

Continuing education and recertification are required to maintain a certification in good standing and maintain your efficiency in current practices, and update your training to new technology and industry trends.

Certifications are either exam based or assessment and exam based. Assignments, projects, hands on activities and exam scores all play a part in the achievement of your certification.

The certification course developed and used in conjunction with this book, upholds standards defined both by the mainstream industry and the faith based community. It has been designed specifically with the faith based community in mind to address the specialized needs of that community and its audience.

**CHAPTER ONE**

# EVENTS AS MINISTRY

IN THOSE DAYS THERE WAS NO KING IN
ISRAEL; EVERY MAN DID WHAT WAS
RIGHT IN HIS OWN EYES.

JUDGES 21:25
(AMPLIFIED BIBLE)

This verse of scripture brings to end the book of Judges in the Old Testament of the Bible. The story that precedes this passage speaks of a group of people working to reach a common goal. Their common goal was to prevent the tribe of Benjamin from becoming extinct due to the inability to reproduce without wives, while not breaking an oath taken prohibiting themselves from providing wives for the Benjamite men.

This goal was vitally important to the ultimate survival of the tribe of Benjamin. To this end the larger group devised a strategy to capture wives for the Benjamite men. They thought their plan through, looked for holes in the plan and even conceived contingencies in case the plan hit a snag. And ultimately they did what they set out to do and arrived at their goal of obtaining wives, thereby enabling the tribe to continue its existence through a lineage of children. Great right?

It might seem so at face value. But in reality a few of the laws that had been established for the tribes were bent just a little. The men of Benjamin were instructed to lay in wait and capture the virgin of their choosing during a festival. The larger group prepared for the fathers and brothers of these women to complain of the capture by asking them to comply with the capture for the Benjamite men had not been adequately provided. This event would provide for them and leave you innocent of a crime, ultimately creating a win-win. No one offended the Law set by God and the objective had been met. But what about the virgins captured as wives...

Interesting story, but doesn't this resemble the manner in which many ministries operate within a given church? Every ministry is given the same vision of the Pastor and a mission for the church and those are their marching orders. This information is taken back to the ministry teams and from there everyone sets their minds to the work of the ministry.

However, somewhere down the line things can get a little muddy. Ministry work can become very involved and workers can run into a hiccup for which they make their own provision. Here's a scenario. Let's take three ministries: Ushers, Music and Parking. They all have the Pastor's vision and the church's mission and a specific sphere of responsibility over which to apply these guiding elements.

How can things go wrong? Here is a scenario:

*Sunday morning 11:00 am service: Set to occur in today's service, the presentation of a Citation from the Mayor's office and a selection by a noted national gospel recording artist.*

The ushers ensure that the congregation gets into the building and gets a seat to hear the word go forth and participate in the worship experience. That is their charge and their responsibility. But the sanctuary fills up very quickly with those wanting to hear the gospel artist, so the ushers begin turning people away from the sanctuary.  Unilaterally people are given a church bulletin and sent either to overflow seating or out of the building with an invitation to return on another day. They are operating by the protocol established within the ministry.

Along with those unilaterally turned away are the guest psalmist for the service, who they didn't recognize,  the elected official bringing greetings from the Mayor's office and a person; without an impressive title or fancy attire, who needed to be in church—*any  church*  that Sunday like no other.

Ultimately, after a great deal of back and forth the guest psalmist was allowed to come into the Sanctuary after the Minister of Music was located and came to the lobby to vouch for her and the representative from the Mayor's office was sent around the building to another door for entry. But what happened to that person that needed to **Meet Christ**?

Where is the disconnect?

Let's take a look: The Ushers defend their position by saying we were at capacity and the fire marshal could have shut us down.  We didn't know there was a guest psalmist for this service and the Mayor's people usually come in with the Pastor or someone from his office.

And they are correct.  The fire marshal could have shut down the service if he had shown up and the service was overcrowded, but did the Ushers alert the Parking ministry or the Greeters that the sanctuary was nearing capacity so members could be directed immediately toward overflow seating rather than going through unnecessary changes?

*Did the music ministry let the Ushers know that a
prominent recording artist would be at the service
and would probably draw non-member followers to
the service resulting in larger numbers for that service
than usual?*

*Did the Administrative office confirm with the Mayor's
people regarding their appearance and give
instructions on where and when to arrive so they
could be seated properly?*

I am equally sure that if the Music Ministry, or the
Administrative Office or Parking and Transportation
were questioned, they would each fully defend their
position by stating that they did everything they were
supposed as it pertained to their ministry duties.

If Parking didn't know there were going to be more
people how could they plan for the increase? The music
ministry was tasked with contacting the artist,
identifying a date that worked and taking care of the
musical needs of the artist, not with what the artist told
the public on a local radio station or on their website
which resulted in additional attendance.

Everyone was working in their ministry but alas, within
a *ministry vacuum* and ultimately not only did each
ministry miss the mark, the greater objective was
missed as well. Remember that person that needed to
get to church on this Sunday, like no other? What
happened to that person? Did they get a seat? Did they
hear a word that may have spoken to their situation? Or
did they have yet another disappointment at a time
when they felt they just couldn't handle another
setback?

A moment was missed. The opportunity for someone to
hear a word that may have been life changing was
abandoned.

The ability to allow ministry to go forth while creating an environment in which things are efficiently orchestrated, thereby allowing for the events' ultimate objective to be reached, becomes YOUR ministry in this case.

How do you do that?

What is missing from the above scenario? It's the same thing that was missing in Judges 21. It's the implementation of a series of checks and balances specific to your organization. Back in the book of Judges the Law was clear and there was a King who oversaw the running of the land and corrected those stepping outside the boundaries of the law. This king also maintained the status quo which prevented individuals from taking matters into their own hands and interpreted the best outcome for all the parties involved. The King operated as the check and balance. Now I by all means do not want anyone reading this to think there should be a King in each ministry, we have too many issues with titles as it stands, however mastering the global oversight of duties is the key to your being a royal blessing to your church's larger ministry.

> *"Your objective is not to run roughshod through ministries of the church changing everything they do."*

## KNOW YOUR LANE

In learning to competently operate within the parameters set before you, you allow ministry to go forth. Those parameters are not always stacked in your favor especially at the beginning. But your ability to operate effectively and consistently will eventually show others that your processes do hold water and should be considered, if not adhered to, for the overall success of the event.

***Observation*** is as big a part of what you do as is ***Action***. Your objective is not to run roughshod through the ministries of the church changing everything they do.

You have the ability in ministry to develop a track record. Every worship service, every concert, annual conference or banquet is another opportunity in front of the same audience to prove yourself and develop a reputation of excellence. This reputation of excellence should infiltrate the very fiber of the overall ministry and become the standard, not hoped for, but expected.

The Ministry Event Manager (MEM) is a designation afforded someone who takes a practical look at the execution of ministry through varying outlets and to orchestrate their coexistence for the greater good of the Kingdom.

Throughout this project we will be looking at practical means to achieve goals and attempt to unblur the lines when it comes to the execution of ministry functions. The establishment of *standard operating procedures* with checks and balances requires the ***buy-in*** of all ministries churchwide to stand. With everyone involved and on the same page, no one ministry acts in a manner that will alienate or overlook the job of another ministry.

**CHAPTER TWO**

# ARE YOU OPERATING OLD OR NEW TESTAMENT MINISTRY?

*"Failures don't plan to fail; they fail to plan."*

-Harvey Mackay

You have heard this quote time and time again. But do you realize that preparation is more than making a list and that it often involves feedback and research, in addition to task scheduling. Additionally, preparation involves periodically looking at how you currently do things to ensure that your processes are keeping in line with technology, the needs, habits and lifestyles of those receiving the measure of your ministry.

The basic function of much of the Old Testament is to lay the groundwork for our Christian faith. Many of the processes currently established and followed within our faith based organizations are the same and stem from the teachings found in the Old Testament. They show instances in where there was an unmet need and laid the foundation to meet the need with a solution. But is that the end?

The New Testament however, specifically Romans, Corinthians and Galatians, were written so that we might be able to follow the example of Christ more closely.

How do these two schools of thought apply to the way we execute ministry?

In the simplest terms, I believe that there are certain times and situations that call for new ways to reach a goal.

We are all familiar with the accounts of Jesus being accused of breaking the Sabbath by healing ((Matthew 12:10; Mark 3:2, John 9:14–16) and by plucking and eating the heads of grain (Luke 6:2). Jesus knew and understood the laws established in the Old Testament. I am not a biblical scholar but is my belief that his intention was not to overhaul the law. He possessed a reverence for the law but on certain occasions saw that a situation presented itself that required a different approach.

Does this mean that we "go rogue" at every instance in which we deem an alternate course of action is required? Of course not, but it does introduce a new way of thinking. We should be contemplating and taking into account the following;

*Are the processes currently in place, the best most effective method of reaching our objectives and our people?*

*Are the processes currently in place, able to keep up with the new objectives our Pastor would like to meet?*

That is what I mean by New Testament thinking. The Old Testament both in the Bible and in the life of your church plays an important role defining who you are and where you come from. A re-evaluation of "the way things are currently" to ensure you are maximizing your resources and garnering the desired results for your Pastor, your congregation and your greater community is always beneficial.

Too often leaders want to know what they have to **DO**, rather than taking the time to examine the scope of the project and understand the ramifications of their actions *before* they move. We are talking about reputation building. Do it right and you are a superstar, do it wrong or treat it lightly and you may never get a second opportunity.

LISTENING is probably the most underused tool of many leaders and planners, because we want to show how capable we are to <u>achieve</u> the task at hand.

*We have two ears and one mouth so that we can listen twice as much as we speak.*

—Epictetus

*"If speaking is silver, then listening is gold."*

—Turkish Proverb

*"Listen a hundred times; ponder a thousand times; speak once."*

– Turkish Proverb

We are a results based society. Getting to the end and seeing the result is the manner in which many of us have been programmed.

The story you read in the last chapter is an Old Testament recount. How many of our faith based organizations are still operating solely with Old Testament procedures. Yes, our mindsets and our messages may indeed be New Testament but it is amazing to see the Old Testament procedures still in play. And the reason for this? Well, because, for the most part, *it has always been done this way.* This is the way the people before us did it and it has worked for this long so we can continue to do it this way. It is easier to do it this way than deal with the backlash that normally accompanies CHANGE.

But how well is it working for your organization?

Are you merely "*getting through*" services and events or are you "**Sailing Through**" with flying colors?

I propose to each of you to take this simple New Testament philosophy as I have proposed it and apply it to the way ministry around you is currently operated.

We will implement the use of a simple and familiar word from the New Testament as an acronym.  A.C.T.S.

A.C.T.S. stands for:

**A**scertain

**C**alculate

**T**ailor

**S**teer

The book of Acts is said to tie the Gospels of the New Testament to all of the other books in the New Testament. This is not unlike your task to tie together the efforts of all the independent ministries to each other and the main event or service at hand.

Let's take a look at *our* New Testament book of A.C.T.S.

**CHAPTER THREE**

# ASCERTAIN

## CLARIFY YOUR GOALS

This is a step overlooked by far too many people and not given much consideration until there is a deliverable i.e. a completed event, and the response to your efforts is somewhat...lackluster.

Goals come to mind once you are hearing what could be considered nitpicky grievances, comments that seemingly hack away at the effort put forth by yourself and your team. Well, whether nitpicky or not, you would have better understood the expectation of your client if the time had been taken to come to a mutual understanding of what was important to the client.

Many planners, or leaders, want a beautiful event or a well publicized event or a smoothly run event. Perhaps your client, or Pastor, really just wants an event that is well attended by the right audience. Do you know? Have you clearly incorporated your client's desired outcomes into your planning process?

This is the information gathering stage. Ask the questions and listen, *don't assume* you know the answers. You may be surprised to find that people are often not completely clear or in agreement as to owning responsibility for certain tasks. This blurring of the lines is another factor that leads to ineffective operation and the ever present finger pointing.

## WHAT ARE YOU BEING BROUGHT IN TO DO?

*Identify deliverables.*
Is it a piece of the pie or the entire pie? Be clear and listen to the request rather than just taking the ball and running away with it, only to be complaining about what **THEY** gave you to do, should you run into complications.

*Identify key people/participants.*
Who is currently involved in the process? Who should be involved in the process? Who is making the final decisions? The use of a RASCI chart (Figure 1) or matrix is an apt method for being able to keep track of these relational items and ensure everyone on your team is clear on what information needs to be funneled to whom and with what priority. This is not a new tool but one very helpful as you being to work with larger events. Depending on the project, the stakes for many of the events on which you will become involved can get very high and you will find that risk management is a crucial and strategic tool for maneuvering your way toward success.
Let's decrypt it. RACI is an acronym for Responsible, Accountable, Consulted and Informed.

| RACI Definitions | |
|---|---|
| **R** Who is Responsible | The person who is *assigned* to do the work |
| **A** Who is Accountable | The person who makes the *final decision* and has the *ultimate ownership* |
| **C** Who is Consulted | The person who must be consulted *before* a decision or action is taken |
| **I** Who is Informed | The person who must be informed that a decision or action *has* been taken |

Figure 1

The key to the RACI chart (Figure 2) is to ensure that every task has a person fulfilling the A - Accountable role. By understanding the roles of those in the organization, you can keep the channels of communication open and everyone informed based on their need or desire to have information and updates. The chart will also assist in your not forgetting anyone that should be a part of the process.

| RACI | | | | | |
|---|---|---|---|---|---|
| Activity | Pastor Smith | Rev. Brown | Min. Wilson | Bro. Carroll | Sis. Waters |
| Sponsorship | A | R | I | I | I |
| Marketing | I | A | R | C | C |
| Volunteers | I | A | R | C | C |
| Operations | A | I | I | R | I |

Figure 2

## IDENTIFY SPECIFIC OUTCOMES:

*What are the desired goals and objectives?*
Being clear on what your client is hoping to achieve will be paramount to success.

Agree on the measures for success and how each will be captured (an on-time start, number of attendees, number of new members, number of acts performing, number of media hits, etc.)

Identify constraints associated with the event (budget, duration, capacity, concurrent activities)

Ask questions to determine if known constraints on the event will impact the desired success of the event. Everything must be feasible. It's easy to say we want 1000 people to attend the event, but if you only have the space for 250, some other things need to be done in order to meet that objective.  Do you have the available resources to make that happen?

## IDENTIFY THE PROBLEMS BEFORE THE SOLUTIONS:

Putting the problems on the forefront and calling a spade a spade is a wise starting point.

**Note:**
*I did not say blaming any one
person or group for a problem.*

As a  group, ownership of your reality is paramount, then as a team you can work together to address the issues with strategic solutions.

## THE EVENT TEAM:

So who are the key stakeholders and participants in the event that need to be plugged into the RASCI chart we spoke of previously? Do you know who you need to be in communication with and why? Within each organization and even each event, the team is going to change. Familiarize yourself with the groups, departments or ministries that play a part in the running of the organization. Some team members to consider:

*Yourself and your core team:*
It will be necessary for certain events to create a short term team to work on execution and planning. This need not be a new ministry but a planning committee which can be disbanded upon the successful execution of the event. If the number of events is large and ongoing the development of a new ministry may very well need to be established.

*The Client:*
The Pastor is normally your client, but as more and more organizations are implementing Event Management departments, other ministries may become your client. They will be seeking your expertise to assist in making their ventures more successful.

Now think about the groups that operate within your organization that you may be working with:

- Administrative staff
- Acolytes
- Adjutants
- Audio
- Caterers
- Dancers
- Deaf Signers
- Drivers
- Floor directors
- Hospitality and Greeters
- Housekeeping
- Intercessors
- Ushers
- Ministers
- Maintenance
- Makeup and Hair stylists
- Musicians and Singers
- Photography
- Pulpit Staff
- Security
- Speakers
- Operations
- Video

As you see the list can become very large, very quickly. Your interaction with some of these areas may be limited, but your lack of interaction with any one of them could wreak havoc on your entire event.

Additionally, don't forget the *"just need to be informed"* partners.

- Parents
- Trustees and the Board
- Local Police and Fire Departments
- Media (consider both internal and external)
- Surrounding Community

## WHO ARE YOU REPORTING TO?

Learn the lines of communication. Get the appropriate information to the appropriate person. This will serve you better than trying to show all the other stakeholders the hard work you are doing.

If you don't have the credit card, you don't have the final decision. Know who does have the final decision and what the correct procedure is for getting an approval. Is it a form that needs to be run up the chain and returned, is there a board approval process for certain amounts and if so, when do they meet and what is the amount that needs their approval? When are checks cut? Is there a PO system in place?

Understanding the process will allow you to complete your project with a minimum of unforeseen delays.

## WHAT IS **NOT** UNDER YOUR PURVIEW?

Are you the *visionary* or the *executor* of the vision? This goes back to what you are commissioned to do. Understand that a part of the responsibility lies on you to ask the correct questions in these areas. Leave nothing to assumption. Being able to avoid stepping on anyone's toes during the process may be the thing that sets YOU apart from everyone else.

## How Will you Communicate?

Telephone, email, face to face?  What works for both parties? Are you sending emails to someone who only checks them when you call and say *"Have you checked your email?"*  Are your voicemail messages piled up because your contact relies on email? Figure this out in advance. Your communication is not information unless it is received.

## When Will you

## Provide Follow Up?

> "Your *communication* is not *information* unless it is received."

This is huge. Set deadlines for delivering updates and to keep those who you report to, in the loop. If you should encounter a setback and everyone has been in the loop all along, you are less likely to be seen as dropping the ball and it is more apt to be seen as something unforeseen.

*When will you get what you need in order to keep the process moving forward?*

The update process is a two way street as well. If the client sees a delay in being able to provide you with certain resources at a given time, you will be able to show how the process may be delayed or to work with them to reorganize the plan and work around the delay, keeping the greater project on schedule.

## WHAT ARE THE BOUNDARIES FOR CONTACT?

Honor the hierarchy of your organization. Despite having pre-established relationships with other stakeholders, send information up the chain appropriately.

## WHEN DO YOU WORK?

Are evenings, weekends and Sunday's open for you to be contacted? What about early mornings or late nights? Remember often your client wants to work with you *when **they** aren't working for someone else.* Be sure to set clear boundaries so that you don't become a 24/7 outlet. Be flexible but clear.

## WHAT ARE THE PERSONALITY TYPES OF THE PEOPLE YOU ARE WORKING WITH?

Many, many people remark to me that I must have the patience of a saint to do what I do. I work closely with a large number of church members, and volunteers.

What I have found is that it's not an elevated patience level that aids me (I am actually quietly impatient...) but rather an understanding of the personalities of those with whom I work. Once I get a feel for someone's personality, I can adjust how I interact with them. It much easier for me to be flexible if it will make someone else more comfortable. Furthermore, my flexibility will allow them to provide what I need in order to get my job done.

I try to observe as much about them as I can. Are they quiet and timid? Are they unable to make or commit to a decision? Micro Managers, Procrastinators?

### How do they process information?

Are they the type to respond to your question with a stream of subsequent questions before answering your original question? Do they need to bounce everything off of someone else? Do they need to exhaust every available option first? Do they need a few hours or days to "chew on" an idea before making a decision? Are they visual and need to "see" every option? Once I understand this about a person it allows me to provide information to them in a manner and in a timeframe that will allow them to work within their personality's comfort zone.

### Have they ever done this before?

If this is a recurring event that has been done numerous times, perhaps your mission is not to do it bigger and better but assure that it takes places smoothly and meets its objective. Not every event needs a complete overhaul. There is often a viable reason things have been done in one manner or another in the past. Quell this information before throwing everything out to do it your way.

### Am I usurping anything from my volunteers?

If this is an event that has been done in the past, is your contact ready to release or share the reins? The church setting is a very different dynamic than a corporate setting. Many, many volunteers feel a strong sense of worth from the work they perform at the church. What is currently working at the organization and how can you build on those things? Be careful in how you work with someone who may feel as though they are being pushed out, whether that is perception or fact. You have an opportunity to teach and change a person's outlook or hone a skill set in them. Your job is ministry as well. Keep that in mind.

*Learn how to laugh.*

Keeping an atmosphere that is light and safe for input and contribution is paramount to getting things accomplished. Participants need to feel as though they are involved in a process that is conducive to getting things accomplished and that they will be heard.

*Invite the squeaky wheel*

Within the world of church volunteers, you are rarely without a few members who have a strong opinion on the way things should be. These same individuals will also have opinions on why things are wrong and who isn't doing something properly. Yes , they are naysayers. However, they pay attention and have been involved in the process for a significant amount of time. Working **WITH** them and ultimately getting buy-in **FROM** them is a huge win for the group. It may not be easy and you may not initially be successful but if you are looking to identify specific problems in the current processes these people can be gems.

*Be led by the vision, not by the budget.*

We will talk a great deal about budgets as we go forward, but I always want you to think of the budget as a means to keep things on track but never to allow the budget to override the vision. If you cannot accomplish the activities you desire because the budge won't allow, keep brainstorming, do not stop the process. Throwing money at a project is not what we are here to do and is not good stewardship. Your objective needs to be accomplished and in the words of my Dad, *"There is always more than one way to skin a cat."* Come up with your grandest ideas and then determine how to tailor them to both fit your budget and allow the vision to be fulfilled.

### Neither Good nor Bad...Just Ideas.

They say there is no such thing as a bad idea but let's take it one step further and establish as a ground rule that conversely there is also no such thing as a good idea. At this point its not about good or bad, but about having resource information with which to work. Every idea that is contributed to the process is valuable whether it is ultimately implemented or not. The most important thing is getting the ideas onto the table as contributions.

### Mix it Up. Inspire Participation.

If your meetings are always held on the second Tuesday of the month in Room 24 at 6:00 pm everyone knows what to expect. What if you were to mix it up? Change the location, the day of the week to better immerse the group into the process. Change the experience of the "meeting". What if choir rehearsal was held at the gym and everyone sang while jogging to build endurance this week? What if you reenacted the process and had the ushers stand in line outside one evening in the cold as some parishioners may have to do on a winter Sunday morning. Do you think that the way they looked at the situation might change? Move out of the classroom and into the area where service occurs. Keep it interesting, keep it personal and allow the participants to know that every meeting will be an experience.

**CHAPTER FOUR**

# CALCULATE

Information is key. Get all the information you can and learn to catch clues to things that may be important but not necessarily articulated. Take all the information that you have "ascertained" and begin to calculate your resources.

Resource is a broad word that we need to look at in the terms of physical things like paper and pens but also in less tangible terms like time, space and volunteers.

## WHAT IS THE BUDGET?

This is the most difficult question to get answered. The minute you receive an answer is the moment your client wishes they had given a lower number. Make sure before moving forward that the budget is feasible. If not, what will give? What can be scaled back? Can certain attributes be omitted completely? What should be deemed "Must Have" and what should be parked on the "Wish List"?

Working with a budget can be very subjective and your job is to take some of the emotion out of the process. That is the beauty of numbers, they are what they are. All budgets total 100%. If you are able to allocate a percentage of the budget to each cost associated with your project the budget will draft itself. By giving each line item a specific percentage of the budget you will be able to very quickly provide a draft budget for the event. Once the draft budget is run, it can be shared with your stakeholders. Everyone can then accurately determine if the numbers "shake out" or need to be massaged. It's not enough to have one large ballpark figure. Some things may be more important than others for a specific event. By seeing how the numbers actually shake out in each category you will have a guide as you move forward, helping to identify vendors and services which will save you time.

Be sure to get a sign off on the final agreement of the budget and the complete scope of work at the *beginning* of the process to avoid misunderstandings. Distribute copies to those core members needing it, your budget need not be for general consumption.

> *Side note: If you are not a volunteer or ministry leader, but rather an outside event planner (vendor) contracted by the organization, make sure you have contracts that are easily manipulated or customized so that there is no delay in the start of the process based on you. More often than not there will be an attorney involved in the contract negotiation portion of the project rather than anything being handled by persons at the ministry level.*

## WHERE WILL THIS PROJECT TAKE PLACE?

Will you be identifying an offsite venue? If onsite, what space or spaces will be required? How long will you need use of each space? Is there a process for reserving space internally? What is the capacity of each space and will it accommodate your projected attendance numbers?

## WHEN WILL THIS PROJECT TAKE PLACE?

Is the date currently available? Is there enough lead time to complete the project, given the scope of work to be done? Is there anything else going on  that will compete with this event?

## WHO IS HOSTING THE EVENT?

Is this an internal event or an event hosted by another organization of people that are leasing space on your campus? Is the event churchwide for all members or driven by a particular ministry for a specific subset of the congregation?

## HOW MANY ATTENDEES ARE EXPECTED?

Are you basing your number on  previous activities? Organization size? or other factors?  If this number is merely a desire, and not based on any of the above criteria, are there marketing efforts and budgets included in the plan to support garnering this type of attendance? Big numbers are not always the best answer. You need to be able to EFFECTIVELY reach those that you anticipate.

## WHAT IS THE FORMALITY OF THE EVENT?

Will the event be a casual picnic? High service? Formal banquet?  Venue choice and décor will play a part in the formality.   The price of your ticket can also be manipulated based on the formality of the event. Are there colors for the event? Is there a theme?

## WHAT IS THE CLIENT'S VISION FOR THE END RESULT?

You want to be able to meet or exceed the expectation of the client.  What better way than to see what they see? Are there any pre-conceived notions about the event that you need to know? Has this not gone well before?  Was this someone else's pet project in the past?  Has it always been done the same way with lackluster or declining results? Understand the expectation for the end result at the beginning of the process and use it as a guide as you move forward.

## WHAT DOES A BUDGET LOOK LIKE?

I am less concerned with what format you use for a budget than I am with the information you account for in the budget, which is paramount. Every service has a cost and you need to understand clearly how that cost is being accounted for whether sponsorship, barter, cash, etc. Here is a sample:

**Audio/Visual & Technical -** *(vendor name)*
> Includes external sound system, mics, cd music piped-in, set-up, delivery, staff on site for 2 hours

**Catering & Beverage -** *(vendor name)*
> Tray-passed hors d'oeuvres____ @ $/per person
> Dinner ___ @ $/pp. includes salad, main course, dessert
> Beverage service ___@ $/pp including glassware and staffing
> Staffing, service charge and tax for meals

**Design & Décor -** *(vendor name)*
> ___floral centerpieces @ $/each for buffet area, # centerpieces @ $/each for dinner tables

**Entertainment -** *name of group*
> Student jazz ensemble for cocktail reception

**Facilities & Internal Services**
> Event manager - prep, load-in, event, strike
> Audio/Video - setup hours and event stand-by
> Custodial services

**Parking/Transportation**
> Attendants - ___ @ $/hour for 3 hours

Signage -  parking/pedestrian signs
## Photography/Videography
Includes digital buyout package and 2 hours of photography
## Postage & Mail Processing
Mailroom processing - stuffing, stamping, labeling
## Printed Materials - *(vendor name)*
Design fee - invitation
Invitation - 1000 pcs. (panel card, reply card, and map)
## Publicity/Marketing
Newspaper ad - one 1/2 page ad @ $/per ad
Radio spots
## Rentals - *(vendor name)*
Cocktail area - standup and sit down tables, chairs, linens, glassware
Guest seating - 66" rounds, Chiavari chairs, linens, service and glassware
## Security/Safety
2 plain-clothes officers @ $/hour for # hours
Fire Marshal services
## Signage (event signage)
General event - registration etc.
## Supplies & Miscellaneous
Nametags, mailing labels, miscellaneous supplies
## Venue - *name of venue*
Venue rental fee - # days @ $/day
Venue staffing charges - crew, custodial, stage manager, etc
## Miscellaneous Contingency - 10% of total budget

TOTAL: $ =======

Immediately upon looking at the budget you will see items that can be donated or sponsored. You can also begin your discussions on which items can be handled in house and which items will be best suited to have an outside vendor come in and provide the service. All of these decisions will be driven by the scope of the event.

**Chapter Five**

# Tailor

Tailoring the event is the "tweaking" or the fashioning of the overall experience for its intended audience. There are a few items you need to keep in mind as you look at each event in its planning phase to ensure the core audience receives the intended message, making the event worthwhile.

The tailoring of the event will represent the details that will ultimately separate events hosted by your organization from the same type of event hosted by another organization at another location.

What is it about your organization that sets you apart from everywhere else? What do you do differently? What's your spin? Notice I didn't say what is *"better"*. There is a reason your members are your members and not members somewhere else. Those same attributes may very well appeal to others when they are given the opportunity to come in contact with you.

As you tailor each event, be true to who you are as an organization. You will never successfully be all things to all people. It's also impossible to be effective while attempting to be all things to all people. Your strengths lie in your knowing who you are as an organization.

Is the age demographic of your church older and you would like to be able to attract younger people into the congregation? You need to tailor specific events and specific messages that come from your organization to resonate with a younger demographic. This does not mean replace the message coming from your pulpit, this means create an organizational message that will speak to the younger demographic without alienating your core group.

There is a formula that I learned a while back as somewhat of a litmus test for the planning of a project.

For sake of this conversation you are given three options;

- **FAST,**
- **CHEAP**
- **GOOD**

You have the choice of using only two out of the three options. Quite a predicament this presents huh? If you choose *Cheap* and *Good*, your process will not be **Fast**. If you choose *Good* and *Fast* the process will not be **Cheap** and if you settle for *Fast* and *Cheap* the process will not be **Good**. Think about this as you implement and fine tune your events.

## EXPECTANCY:

What are you planning for this event that will make people want to come? Are you able to draw from a theme and create activities that uphold the purpose of the event? What have you created that will be able to send your message out to the attendees in a number of different fashions. Not everybody "*gets it*" the same way. For one person it may be a visual cue, for another it may be audible for a third it may be through something they can touch. Communicating your information effectively will impact attendance numbers.

## HOSPITALITY:

How will you prepare for your attendees and how will you treat them once they are in your presence? Do you want them to feel welcome? Involved? At ease? Expectant? You set the stage for them the moment they walk into the experience you have created for them. If there is chaos going on, that is the experience you are setting. Making sure your frontline is prepared is crucial. Keep in mind the pace of the audience. If preparing for Seniors the pace of the event may be very different than if you are preparing for a group of youth who need more quick paced transitions between activities. Meeting the needs of your audience within the parameters you have set within your event is paramount. If you put guests outside on a sunny day, be sure you have fans and water to take care of them. If you are hosting a two hour recital, ensure you have adequate seating for everyone where they can see and hear what is occurring on the stage.

> *Good*
>
> *Fast*
>
> *Cheap*
>
> *Pick only Two.*

## SETTING:

Allow the environment to set the stage for the experience you have created. Give some thought to keeping your guests engaged in the experience you have built have and encourage them to be willing and active participants. Setting the scene often involves more than just décor. It could be the use of video or audio. It might be an actor speaking to small groups. Give some thought to your theme and ideas may present themselves.

## SUBSTANCE:

Whether it's food or a sermon or a song make sure it's appealing. The substance is the core of the event. This is the work of the programming arm of the event. Perhaps this task lies on the shoulder of the Pastor, Minister of Music or other ministry leader. By working on the logistic areas of the event, your programmer can focus on the content, strengthening the core of the event. If all goes correctly, the core of the event should be the only thing the programmer has to be concerned with, relying on the belief that everyone else is doing their jobs to maximum effectiveness. Keep in mind though that the programmer needs to be on their game as well and in tune with the audience.  What is going on in the everyday life of the audience for this particular event? Content needs to be relevant and again meet the member where they are. Focus on the majority and not the fringe.  No one can effectively be all things to all people, as we have stated, but if you meet the majority you can at least give the fringe something to think about and who knows they may bend your way to learn more.

## INTERACTION:

Is there an opportunity for engagement? Having people sitting looking at a speaker is not always the most exciting experience. Interaction can be created by both the planners of the event and the programmer. What are the ministries within your organization that can be tapped into to further the interaction with those attending the event? Can props be brought in specifically for an event to heighten the interaction experience?  For instance bringing in a rented Moon Bounce for a children's event can send the experience through the roof for your children's ministry. Even something as simple as a whistle or an inexpensive flag for each participant can make the event interactive if incorporated into the program.

## FELLOWSHIP:

How will you let your guests know that you would like to have them back? Specifically in the faith based community, once you reach a person, regardless of the avenue, you would like to foster a relationship that includes their return.  What are you doing at every encounter to foster a feeling of fellowship? If they had an enjoyable experience at this event, what other events occur regularly that may be as appealing?

Keeping each of these attributes at the forefront of your planning process will increase both the effective execution of the event as well as the anticipated success of the event. You have the base infrastructure of your plan and the beauty is that once this is completed, it can be replicated over and over again, without starting from square one. With a periodic or  annual re-evaluation of the process and minor adjustments as the overall ministry grows and evolves, your process will grow with the organization and remain New Testament ministry and not relapse into prior Old Testament thinking.

**CHAPTER SIX**

# STEERING

This is the area, that I personally have the fiercest respect for and where many, many people drop the ball. Delivery. Making it happen. It's all or nothing at this point. Game day, Show time.

## *What are you going to do?*

This is the area that separates the *"Planners"* from the *"Doers"*. This is where the rubber meets the road and all the titles get thrown out of the window, drop the clipboards honey: You. Must. Deliver.

Each and every engagement is an opportunity for a "God Moment". You are responsible and accountable to approach as each interaction as such. If you knew Jesus was visiting your location, in person, on a given day and time you would bring you're **A**-game. You would be full of energy and motivated to provide an exceptional experience. You would check and double check with each and every person involved. You would understand everything that needs to happen and have a plan for how it will be executed and have a back up as well. You would have extra hands on deck, just in case... After all, this is for Jesus.

Correct me, if I am wrong, but isn't the purpose of every worship service to invoke His presence? Isn't Jesus invited into your worship each and every time? So why do we allow mediocre work and efforts to become the norm?

> *"Our decisions, attitudes, and behaviors are determined by either one of two things.....external pressures or internal principles."*
>
> John MacArthur

What is driving you to have a great event?  Should it matter if there is an acknowledged VIP or is the body of Christ enough of an audience? Excuses for lackluster execution are useless from the choir whose musician didn't show up or the artist whose track doesn't play. They are useless to the speaker who didn't get picked up from the airport or who can't run his computer presentation through your existing system.

Brilliance manifests and the difference becomes clear when, despite the obstacles,  the choir sings a cappella and blows it out of the water and the artist sings fluidly to the playing of the  house organist and the speaker goes forth with the word because; they know their craft without the use of their notes.

> *"Things work out best for those who make the best of the way things are."*
>
> John Wooden

Not fulfilling the obligation is not an option.  Blaming a poor execution on the things that didn't happen is not an option. It's the event that happens despite... Despite late flights, despite technical difficulties, despite missing members, despite lack of confirmation. What do we call that?... A Testimony.

Excuses are also useless to the client to whom you are looking to for payment or to the Pastor who you are hoping will continue to implement your plans throughout the ministry.

There is a saying that reads along the lines of:

*"Excuses are tools of the incompetent.*
*They build monuments of nothingness*
*and bridges to nowhere.*
*Those who use them seldom*
*accomplish anything.*
*Therefore have... No Excuses".*

Author Unknown
Poor Richard's Almanac

Get it done.  Plan A. Plan B. Use your husband, wife or kids, Call in a favor, Lose some sleep, pay it out of your pocket.

> *"Call in a favor, Lose some sleep, Pay it out of your pocket.*
>
> *Just do it."*

Just do It.    *Why?*

**Because it's your reputation  on the line.**

*"Failure is not an option. It is a nagging reality that keeps you focused".*
                                    Joe Clark

Which would you rather hear?

*That power outage really threw a monkey wrench into the concert so many people left early without hearing any music.*

Or...

> *What great thinking to have had the piano moved upstairs. It was worth it to pay the moving fee so the artist could play acoustically while the power was restored. He really got to connect with the crowd and give a once in a lifetime performance.*

Steering  is a global activity and to be able to steer effectively you have to be able to view the process from a vantage point that is global and be confident in making decisions with an understanding of the global repercussions.  If you are bogged down being the butcher, the baker and the candlestick maker you will never be able to see globally.

This starts with your ability to work with people. This is a skill set you must develop and continue to hone. You must be able to utilize the resource pool of people you have at your disposal.  That means, in most cases, meeting them where they are rather than immediately trying to get them to change and adapt to where you are, that is a recipe for mutiny.

It is understood that in most cases you are working with volunteers who may be accustomed to performing one specific task.  If they are proficient at that task utilize them, but always keep your eye out for traits that will make someone whose performance is lackluster in one area shine in another area.  This will become vitally important as your events grow larger in scope and occurrence.

Your job, from your global perch is to test as many scenarios as possible.  What would happen if... What will we do if...Looking into the most probable situations and running through possible alternatives will allow you to salvage an event if something should go awry.

No one on the outside knows the plans you have worked during the span of the planning process so if one leg of the event takes a turn and last minute changes or substitutions are made they will never known by the public. You will be able to maintain the fluidity of the event which is important.

There is a term that I use within my own companies; "flawless logistic execution". It's what we strive for.    My job is a technical one out in the main stream world. I find that when we are able to maintain the logistical prowess over an event we open up the ability to bring in a human factor. When things are running smoothly and according to a well thought out plan, we have the opportunity to interact with more people and find out how they are enjoying the experience.    These moments make an enormous difference to those in attendance. You have the opportunity to cater to a specific need and make someone feel appreciated.    This is a guarantee rave in your favor.    I don't think anything can replace the personal touch. Hearing a grievance and fixing it means the world to people. Sometimes it's the "check-in" to make sure things are going well for those in attendance. Striving for flawless logistic execution is always possible even if the state of perfection is not attained.

**CHAPTER SEVEN**

# TAKE IT TO CHURCH

In this chapter let us take a look at a number of different ministry events and identify common threads as well as hot buttons and red flags that should be on your radar screen.

As mentioned earlier, your view must be global. You no longer have the luxury of looking at things from just one viewpoint. Everyone's viewpoint must be incorporated. While some ministries do a good job of this, many others as of yet, do not. They develop their plans in a vacuum and it takes a lot of trial and unfortunate error to make changes and get on the right track.

Being proactive is the goal. Operating from a reactive standpoint, does allow change to occur but usually at a much higher cost. Being reactive normally leaves casualties and missed opportunities. There is then the thought, IF we had known this would happen, THEN we *would have* done something differently.

With new tactical skills under your belt, the infrastructure for solid event basics is now in place and you're ready to go. Right? Not exactly. When working in ministry, as we have said over and over, there are a number of additional and specific criteria to be taken into consideration. Most poignantly, the fine line between ministry and merely event planning.

In an effort to file down the sometimes rough edged perspective of "*just doing the business*" and turn this business of event planning into *ministry event management* we need to get to a place of understanding the true dynamic that we are impacting. Let's look at the faith based organization a bit closer.

Starting at the top...

# THE PASTOR:

> [10]*He Who descended is the [very] same as He Who also has ascended high above all the heavens, that He [His presence] might fill all things (the whole universe, from the lowest to the highest).*
>
> [11]*And His gifts were [varied; He Himself appointed and gave men to us] some to be apostles (special messengers), some prophets (inspired preachers and expounders), some evangelists (preachers of the Gospel, traveling missionaries), some pastors (shepherds of His flock) and teachers.*
>
> [12]*His intention was the perfecting and the full equipping of the saints (His consecrated people), [that they should do] the work of ministering toward building up Christ's body (the church).*
>
> Ephesians 4:10-12
> (Amplified Bible)

The vision and direction for your organization will stem from the Pastor. Whether he or she is Reverend, Doctor, Reverend Dr., Bishop, Elder, or Apostle: whether a Co-Pastor or Senior Pastor you must have a clear understanding of where the Pastor is leading. If you are in line with this vision, you will come out on top when leading events under this leadership.

Clearly understanding the Pastor's vision also allows you to assist in the development of ministry projects within your church. As ministries are developing events and fundraisers the continual test of their objectives against the Pastor's vision is a vital litmus test.

Keep in mind as well that your Pastor is a person. What are your Pastor's hot buttons?  What are his baseline expectations? You need to know and understand them. Often times many conflicts come from people not being on the same page.

*For instance, if the Pastor does not like to start a service until he is assured that the First Lady has arrived at the church, then the focus should not be on getting him to start on time, but rather the emphasis should be on assuring that the First Lady's adjutant and driver are in the loop on the start time of an event or service and are adequately planning out their timeline to ensure that the First Lady is prepared to arrive on schedule. She probably has habits of her own, that her support are taking into account as well.  Perhaps the First Lady is not aware that her spouse is actually holding service for her arrival and believes the late start is actually due to awaiting for the arrival of more members.*

Communication, not assumption is key in flushing out where the core of an issue may actually lie.

Back to the Pastor,  does he/she run late? Preach long? Are they keen to services heavy with musical interaction?  Do they stick to a script? Stray widely from a script? Are they a stickler for a timely start and finish of events?

Whatever the answers to these questions, they need to be incorporated into the logistical planning of your event.   If late starts and running long are persistent issues at your location, perhaps the training needs to be done with the attendees?   If they believe that services *always*  start late and this is confirmed by services *always* starting late, there has to be a change in behavior, otherwise you will continue to start late because of them and they will continue to arrive late because of you.

See the conundrum?

Work on instilling timely habits and be the example. It will only take attendees missing something great because they were late to urge them into the mindset of arriving on time. We need to get out of the mindset of "tricking" people into coming early for things. It makes absolutely no sense to penalize those attendees that always arrive on time by making them sit while you wait for those who always arrive late?  Enough with false start times and the like. If they miss it, what a great opportunity for your video ministry to sell CD's and DVD's of the service. Most people arrive late, because they aren't missing anything!! YOU set the standard that events at your church start on time and people will follow.

Set the stage to create the atmosphere within  which your Pastor is most comfortable and can give his very best. Build around him. Once your Pastor is confident that those serving around him, understand his cues, whether they be verbal or physical, he will be able to flow with the under girding  of his ministries bolstering him.

He should be able to subtly drop the lines of a song into his commentary and the instruments should begin to softly play, giving him the option of moving the service into a song should he so desire. If you are a member of the choir and hear the opening strains to a song on which you sing the lead, you should move toward a mike. Yes, it is very possible that you might not be needed to sing. I would rather you go back to your seat without having sung than not being ready to sing and having all eyes on you while you try to graciously make your way down through the choir loft to find a microphone.

All eyes should follow his cues, so that his cues can remain subtle and seamless to the congregation. Movements and anticipated actions should be quick and concise.  It only takes a moment for an opportunity to be lost.  If you are responsible for supplying text to be broadcast on the screens, how long should it take for you to find a scriptural reference once it is called out (in the correct version...)? As you begin to work with your Pastor he will also work with you and prompt you to where he is going and what he would like to do. We must be alert and ready to spring into action.   There are some instances for which we cannot rehearse.

*Most people arrive late, because they aren't missing anything...*

*"When you change the way you see things, the things you see change."*

Anonymous

Communication—Mass Communication is very much the name of the game in managing ministry events. You cannot work in a vacuum and unlike in other corporate type events you may have less autonomy in your efforts. Every part of the process in ministry must be in line.  It's no longer a matter of taking a scope of work,  heading back to your office with your team and bringing back an end result that meets the desired objective. Ministry is the melding of efforts with everyone else to achieve a desired result without necessarily knowing how that result is going to manifest itself or to whom the recipient may be on a given occasion.

## WHO ARE YOU WORKING WITH:

Those behind the scenes of a worship service are many. Event Management Team, Space Allocation Schedulers, Catering, Greeters, Transportation, Parking, Security, Signage Committee, Ushers, Choir, Crisis Management, Musicians, Risk Management, Vending, Housekeeping, Worship Leaders, Altar Workers, Praise Team, Pulpit Workers, Operations, Audio, Video, Adjutants, Drivers, Accountants , Trustees, Church Staff, Public Relations, Media, Ministerial Staff, and the list goes on and on...

Do you know what all of these team members do and when they come on the scene? Do you have a contact sheet with current contact information for all the church's ministries? There are some ministries that impact your services and events who are not even required to show up on the day of service.

The planning of an event is not a new phenomenon. Journey with me back to the very first event ever planned... At least I like to think of it that way. Turn with me in your Bible to the book of Genesis take a look at how it was done back then. Perhaps this can serve as an example for your future events.

# THE FIRST EVENT

Genesis 1:1-31, 2:1 Amplified Bible

**Genesis 1**

¹IN THE beginning God (**PREPARED**, formed, fashioned, and) created the heavens and the earth.⁽ᴬ⁾ ²The earth was without form and an empty waste, and darkness was upon the face of the very great deep. The Spirit of God was moving (**HOVERING, BROODING**) over the face of the waters. ³And God said, Let there be light; and there was light.

*God's first __ACTION__ came __AFTER__ preparing, examining and considering with what he had to work.*

⁴And God saw that the light was good (**SUITABLE**, pleasant) and He approved it; and God separated the light from the darkness.⁽ᴮ⁾ ⁵And God called the light Day, and the darkness He called Night. And there was evening and there was morning, one day.

*The implementation of the first standard operating procedure. It was simple and concise. When there is light, we have Day. When there is darkness, we have Night. It's written down and now we know.*

⁶And God said, Let there be a firmament [the expanse of the sky] in the midst of the waters, and let it separate the waters [below] from the waters [above].    ⁷And God made the firmament [the expanse] and separated the waters which were under the expanse from the waters which were above the expanse. And it was so. ⁸And God called the firmament Heavens. And there was evening and there was morning, a second day.    ⁹And God said, Let the waters under the heavens be collected into one place [of standing], and let the dry land appear. And it was so.

*God saw the need for texture and depth separating water from water, water from sky and land from water. The nuts and bolts of your program once set, will need other amenities to add*
*texture    and depth to the overall event making it comprehensive and give it scope.*

¹⁰God called the dry land Earth, and the accumulated waters He called Seas. And God saw that this was good (**FITTING**, admirable) and He approved it.

*God moved carefully and made sure updates worked with everything already in place, rather than trying to remove what was already given and start over.*

¹¹And God said, Let the earth put forth [tender] vegetation: plants yielding seed and fruit trees yielding fruit whose seed is in itself, each according to its kind, upon the earth. And it was so. ¹²The earth brought forth vegetation: plants yielding seed according to their own kinds and trees bearing fruit in which was their seed, each according to its kind. And God saw that it was good (**SUITABLE**, admirable) and He approved it. ¹³And there was evening and there was morning, a third day.

*Your resources are in the house.   Within your organization are the tools, ingenuity and manpower to achieve the desired goals. Its your job to access your resources and learn what their capabilities are and where they best fit.*

¹⁴And God said, Let there be lights in the expanse of the heavens to separate the day from the night, and let them be signs and tokens [of God's provident care], and [to mark] seasons, days, and years,(C)    ¹⁵And let them be lights in the expanse of the sky to give light upon the earth. And it was so.

*Ministry members: The lights sent to assist the processes already put into place. In the above verses, we already know that light has been separated from darkness, God saw fit to add additional light to be tokens of his care.*

16And God made the two great lights--the greater light (the sun) to rule the day and the lesser light (the moon) to rule the night. He also made the stars.    17And God set them in the expanse of the heavens to give light upon the earth,    18To rule over the day and over the night, and to separate the light from the darkness. And God saw that it was good (fitting, pleasant) and He approved it.    19And there was evening and there was morning, a fourth day.

*The greater Light, the Pastor and the lesser light(s) ministry leaders and staff to continue ministry while the Pastor rests.  The stars are ministry members; shining lights to show others where work is being is being accomplished.*

20And God said, Let the waters bring forth abundantly and swarm with living creatures, and let birds fly over the earth in the open expanse of the heavens.    21God created the great sea monsters and every living creature that moves, which the waters brought forth abundantly, according to their kinds, and every winged bird according to its kind. And God saw that it was good (suitable, admirable) and He approved it.    22And God blessed them, saying, Be fruitful, multiply, and fill the waters in the seas, and let the fowl multiply in the earth.    23And there was evening and there was morning, a fifth day.

*The creation of congregation and community. Created to multiply and inhabit the edifice being operated for God. Everything created has the ability to make an impact. There is a reason for each and every creature, if someone is sent into your sphere of responsibility, be responsible in utilizing their gift.*

[24]And God said, Let the earth bring forth living creatures according to their kinds: livestock, creeping things, and [wild] beasts of the earth according to their kinds. And it was so.  [25]And God made the [wild] beasts of the earth according to their kinds, and domestic animals according to their kinds, and everything that creeps upon the earth according to its kind. And God saw that it was good (fitting, pleasant) and He approved it.

*People, workers, volunteers.  Each one adding to the experience with what they natively bring to the table. Created to show that each of us has an impact on the Kingdom and the creation of opportunities to allow access into that Kingdom for all to enter.*

[26]God said, Let Us [Father, Son, and Holy Spirit] make mankind in Our image, after Our likeness, and let them have complete authority over the fish of the sea, the birds of the air, the [tame] beasts, and over all of the earth, and over everything that creeps upon the earth.[D]    [27]So God created man in His own image, in the image and likeness of God He created him; male and female He created them.[E]    [28]And God blessed them and said to them, Be fruitful, multiply, and fill the earth, and subdue it [using all its vast resources in the service of God and man]; and have dominion over the fish of the sea, the birds of the air, and over every living creature that moves upon the earth.

*The finishing touches to the event.  The Pièce de résistance. The one thing that will take the event from ordinary to extraordinary.  The creation of man was the icing on the cake for God's creation, created to give him praise.*

[29]And God said, See, I have given you every plant yielding seed that is on the face of all the land and every tree with seed in its fruit; you shall have them for food.    [30]And to all the animals on the earth and to every bird of the air and to everything that creeps on the ground--to everything in which there is the breath of life--I have given every green plant for

food. And it was so.

31And God saw everything that He had made, and behold, it was very good (suitable, pleasant) and He approved it completely. And there was evening and there was morning, a sixth day.

**Genesis 2**

1THUS THE heavens and the earth were finished, and all the host of them.

> *Before the doors open on any event we set our hands to, we should be able to reexamine and consider our choices and decisions and feel the very same way.*

So how do we now apply this to our everyday experience within the walls of our own churches? Let's take a look at a few common ministry efforts and how we apply the lessons from the previous passages and the tools we have compiled thus far. By walking through a few of the obstacles one should keep in their sights, you may be able to institute a few quick modifications that will drastically improve the execution of ministry in these areas.

## WORSHIP SERVICE:

You may not currently have the opportunity to participate in the direction of your church's worship service, however don't believe that  will always be the case.  As congregants become savvier and new ministries develop, the worship service too evolves.  More and more churches are incorporating, plays, skits, dance, mime, broadcasts, video and many other elements into the worship service and because most services do not have the option of running longer, they must be scripted to run efficiently.

Normally the biggest retort I get the moment I say *scripted worship services*  is  "You can't quell the Spirit, it's going to do what it's going to do."

I agree completely. Neither you nor I possess the ability to quell the Spirit. The Spirit **IS** going to do what it's going to do. What I am subscribing to is the belief that having a plan for everything *else* is just smart ministry.  The objective here is not to constrain the worship experience, but rather to **open  up**  the opportunities for worship to occur. A well orchestrated, thoughtfully planned out service that takes a turn because the Spirit dictates it be so, is a service that can very easily be brought back on track once that shift has taken place.

Not everyone knows what to do when things take on a life of themselves and this is often felt in the lack of ability to *recover*. However, if ministries are trained in where they are going, they are able to discuss how to maneuver back when needed and not to become an obstacle in the process.

There are certain areas of your church worship services that are informational; announcements, welcome to visitors etc. There are other portions that are worshipful; prayer, altar calls, the invitation to discipleship, Communion etc. Some portions are ritual like the scripture and the benediction. Other portions may be high praise; choir selections, dance ministries, offering. And of course the sermon, the "meat" of the service.

How long do these activities take in your church? Does it vary by service or can you set a watch by them? If you haven't already, take a look at the activities that happen in the worship service at your church and time them. Once you have data that you can work with, you can begin to look at and discuss how the service is currently working and perhaps how it can be improved.

*For instance take a look at the collection of your offering. Is it really feasible in larger churches, to have an offering where all members walk around and personally deposit their offering in a basket? How long does this take? What else is happening at this time? Is there a more efficient method for collecting offering? What about the long observed March of the Ushers to deposit their offering? If you have more than one service, perhaps this ceremonial activity is only performed at the last service rather than at every service.*

Tradition is very important. Keeping the "feel" of your church service is vital to serving the congregation of your church. Keep this in mind as alterations to the service are being considered for implementation and get buy-in from the ministries involved. Simply removing everything is not the option we are suggesting in every case. Take too much away and you will hack away at the essence of who your organization has taken a great deal of time to become.

Knowing the answers to these questions is the key to developing a worship service that ultimately meets the objectives of everyone in attendance.

Congregants get a fully packed service with plenty of stimulus and information, the Pastor sends the message out to the masses, offerings are collected, choirs sing the songs they rehearse, the varying ministries are able to serve the body and an experience with Christ is allowed to occur.

Looking at it from this perspective allows you to also see the holes, as each action depends on the actions of other ministries. Every ministry is equi-important.

*If there is no parking, congregants are late, if there are no seats, congregants are looking for overflow, if ushers are giving directions, they can't seat people, if bulletins aren't folded in advance ushers are running double duty. If the choir doesn't know the name of the sermon, they don't choose an appropriate hymn, or may choose an inappropriate selection. If audio doesn't know when the liturgical dancers are dancing, they don't have music cued. Soloists don't have mikes at the ready. Props aren't moved after skits, and the list goes on and on. However a run sheet, modified for each service, every week, can accommodate every change and be placed in the hands of every ministry that participates in the worship service.*

Think about it,  your Pastor now has complement of ministries that are supporting him and working in their full capacities as they were designed.  Everyone is then poised for God to move mightily. Does that not bring to life the scripture found in Ephesians 3:20 ?

*Now to Him Who, by (in consequence of) the (action of His) power that is at work within us, is able to (carry out His purpose and) do superabundantly, far over and above all that we (dare) ask or think (infinitely beyond our highest prayers, desires, thoughts, hopes or dreams).*

The Amplified Bible

Your Pastor can now focus on reaching not just the people he's been reaching all along, but their children, parents, siblings, co-workers, friends and neighbors... What will that do to the entire ministry at large?  It will grow.  It will be alive and thriving.

Think of it like a car.  If you have a hooptie for a car, you can still get from point A  to point B and back because you know your car.    Whether the issue is brakes or transmission or something else, you don't take it any further than you can trust it to handle. It may be great for going to the store, but you probably wouldn't drive it cross country.  However when you have a car that is maintained and upgraded and serviced regularly, you have the confidence to take it anywhere you desire to go because you trust it.

We can do the same things over and over and have the same outcome or we can grow and take steps to further our development and reach higher heights. The power is within our own hands. What we do with it is up to us.

## ADDITIONAL OPPORTUNITIES FOR SERVICE

*What types of events does your ministry hold?*

- Baptism
- Bible Study
- Book Signings
- CD Recordings
- Children's events
- Communion
- Concerts
- Funerals
- Group Conferences
- Musician/Celebrity Appearances
- Ordination Services
- Picnics
- Plays
- Prayer Vigils
- Rallies
- Seminars
- Weddings
- Worship Service
- Youth Events
- External community events

Your church finds itself with a myriad of services to perform. Some of these services happen routinely every week like your Sabbath worship services, others happen with a great deal of pre-planning and yet others occur very quickly. Whatever the lead time, if you are prepared, each of these services can go off flawlessly.

## FUNERALS:

We know neither not when a funeral will occur nor what the expected attendance of each funeral will bring. Working with the bereaved family is not our objective here, there are ministry and staff persons tasked specifically with that role. Our objective is to have an established procedure in place that can be immediately enacted with one phone call and executed with dignity. It's not about the bells and whistles here it is about the non existence of logistical flubs. What do I mean?

Items like having a sound person available to operate the sound system and microphones who is available during business hours any day of the week. This may be five different people but as long there is one person always available you are covered. The same applies to choir members and musicians willing and available to serve at a day's notice, even if they did not know the deceased. These are seemingly small things that amount to a world of difference to a family during a difficult time in their lives.

## WEDDINGS:

We will discuss this in great detail in a future chapter, but this hopefully once in a lifetime event, means the world to the couple involved and there is only one opportunity to get it right and meet, if not exceed their expectations. It is also a time to refocus on the reason for the gathering, the actual wedding ceremony, not merely the décor, flowers and DIY projects, but most importantly the covenant being entered into by two people.

## PRAYER VIGILS:

Setting the atmosphere on a sacred occasion is as much of a feat as a large theatrical production. A peaceful worshipful environment involves the same attention to detail as a concert, only in reverse. Focusing on the omission of distractions like noise and excessive movement and  preparing appropriate music are all key to the service experience. Corporate prayer is powerful and when ushered in properly is life altering.

## ORDINATION CEREMONIES:

High ceremonial services often culminate major milestones within the life of your congregation. Ordination services are often the most intricately choreographed services in which you will participate. The adherence to tradition and ceremony is strict. But when executed properly the effects are monumental. Expect for the planning of these types of services to be a coordinated effort with a higher body that operates within your faith.  By having a ministry staffed with people trained to execute with excellence the planning of these types of services will astound your congregation. Once you have mastered working together amongst yourselves in a seamless manner, when you afforded the opportunity to work with those outside of your own congregation you will be astounded at how the process flows. You can become the expert of your spaces and work in tandem with those who are solely concerned with the ceremonial pieces of the event.

## CONFERENCES:

These events are usually integrating two distinct types of events. On the one hand there will be mass corporate worship or plenary service to include a keynote speaker and music, much like your Sabbath worship service. In addition there will be many smaller breakout sessions and vendor offerings that will run concurrently. Having a large number of trained volunteers and a tight logistics plan is paramount to a successful conference for the attendance can range from a few hundred to several thousand. These events are normally multi-day events. It is necessary to be able to hit the ground running and to maintain momentum over the course of several days.

## PICNICS AND RALLIES:

These family oriented events are always fun for the entire membership. Casual and inclusive they are the perfect time for fellowship. Whether in recognition of Family and Friends Day, Back to School or any other type of inter-ministry occasion, success is an expected outcome. Plan contingencies for weather of course and ensure the safety of small children and the elderly with added efforts directed at these core groups.

## PLAYS:

Plays have really taken on a huge following in the church, but they are a major undertaking. This is another area where you need to stay in your lane. The production and direction of a play are very different from the execution of a play as a church event. You will not play the role of staging, directing or producing. Your role becomes that of liaison between all of the other ministries that need to interact in order for the play to be presented. You are ensuring there is security and parking, that there are enough seats in the house, ushers, greeters, ticketing services, coat check, catering services, room/space allocation for cast and crew, housekeeping etc. Not as glamorous as when we first started huh? But again this is vitally important to the success of the event. A play or concert is often the perfect opportunity for a potential member to be introduced to your church.

## CONCERTS:

Concerts can be either internal, involving your own home choirs or can involve the leasing of your space by an external group such as a national recording artist.

Developing a concert for an internal choir can prove to be more than just a showcase of the choir's efforts. It is always a major opportunity to introduce new people to your church.  Because the appreciation of music is so widespread, a musical concert is a great invitation to someone that may not regularly attend church or may be searching for a church home.

I am sure you can guess the words I am about to share. When working on a concert "*stay in your lane*". Leave the music selection, interpretation and arrangement to your Music Ministry.  Once they have done this you should have the opportunity to glean from them their vision for the concert.  Is there a theme?  Holiday Cantata? A Cappella Spirituals? Old Time Hymns and Anthems?  What are they wearing?  Choir robes? Festive seasonal colors?  Will they be working in concert with dancers? Will there be an intermission? Will there be an offering?

This type of information will enable you to help promote the concert internally and externally. Design marketing materials, get it listed in the church bulletin, create a skit to promote it, send invitations or postcards out, work on a radio commercial spot.

Where in the program will the offering take place? Will you need the same full complement of ministry on hand as for a  regular worship service. How long will the program last?   Will it be an afternoon or evening function? What dates are available on the church's calendar?  Has the Pastor's calendar been checked for his ability to attend and perhaps emcee?

How can this event be taken up a notch to expand the reach of ministry? Could you invite a local elementary school glee club as your guests and have them sing with the choir on a selection. Is there a local play or gospel artist that will be in town at the time that could make a special appearance?

*Stay in your lane.*
*Learn to work*
***WITH***
*and empower*
*other ministries.*

Another thing to keep in mind within house choirs is the legal use of music. It is important to do things in decency and order and be mindful of copyright laws and the appropriate way to copy, distribute and record music.

Inviting or granting the request of a national recording artist into your church brings with it a different level of management.  It should not necessarily be "heightened", just different.  Every event, service or program at your church should be done to the same level of excellence because each is an opportunity for something far greater than just the event at hand.

Once the negotiation has been settled for the artist be sure you are aware of everything that has been agreed upon.  Travel and lodging for the talent and entourage. Ground transportation from the hotel to your location. Time to be blocked out for rehearsal and sound checks.

Whose equipment is being used? Instruments, sound, video? Is it your house equipment or is an outside company going to be required to meet the need? Dressing rooms? Food. Are there any other acts that will be performing? Scheduling and the use of volunteers will be crucial in this area.

What about publicity of the event? The event will most likely be ticketed however will there be a fee? Free tickets or passes are a great way to control capacity. If a ticket is required for entry once tickets are distributed you know that you are at your seating capacity and can control a situation from getting out of hand.

Security for the event is also paramount. You don't want a Fire Marshal shutting your event down because you are unable to manage the crowd or because you weren't aware of the legal capacity for the building. Do you know the legal capacity for the spaces in your building?

VIP seating needs to be addressed as well and for how long will special seating be available. Will items be sold? Is there a split negotiated for the sale of CD's or t-shirts? Or perhaps the opportunity to sell product in lieu of a performance fee.

As the types of events you have increase, your capacity and manpower to produce these events will need to increase in order to manage the greater complexity of the events. Being able to proficiently handle the events that recur will provide the practical experience, tools and protocols needed to tackle larger events.

**CHAPTER EIGHT**

# THAT VOLUNTEER SPIRIT

## WORKING WITH VOLUNTEERS:

Working with people is a job within itself. Communicating and interacting with multiple personality types and with persons who have an often fierce pride in the responsibility that has been afforded them up until this point can be trying. The manner in which you approach this aspect of ministry will really set the tone for your success.

The dynamics found in the church are a little unusual and follow a hierarchy that is developed over many, many years of things being a certain way.

Change is difficult because it is uncertain, unproven  and uncomfortable. It need not be an open and shut incident. You can massage your way through bringing those along with you willing to take the journey.

I  challenge you start with a change in *your* outlook toward the process of working with people. Understand that many you encounter may not embrace or even be open to change. They not see things the way you do. Creating a viable pool of volunteers will be a key point in the success of your events.

You can look at it from a standpoint of optimism or you can approach it from a stand point of faith. Do you believe that the shifts that you are assisting to implement  are a part of God's will for this ministry?  If so, then believe that the goal will be achieved.

> *15 He said: "Listen, King Jehoshaphat and all who live in Judah and Jerusalem! This is what the LORD says to you: 'Do not be afraid or discouraged because of this vast army. **For the battle is not yours, but God's.***

*2 Chronicles 20:15 (NIV)*

Do not head into your situation with something to prove. You have been empowered to lead, but lead with the humility of a servant. There is a familiar saying:

> *"A leader without followers is merely a guy out taking a walk."*

If God has ordained this season, He will soften the hearts of those with whom you are working. **OR** He won't.

Yes, it is very possible that you will face a group of resistant personalities that refuse to bend and conform. **You** will be developed under the pressure of the situation. Either way it's a win for the Kingdom.

## *WHY CAN'T I USE MY OWN CORE TEAM?*

To that I would counter, why not make *everyone* capable of being on your core team? The more capable and available arms and legs you have at your disposable, the less you run the risk of burning out a small core team. One's dependence on a small resource pool will result in the integrity of the events you oversee diminishing. One of the smartest tools you could assist in creating is a viable, regularly maintained database of volunteers and their skill sets.

Use this opportunity to develop leaders. It will ultimately allow a wider spectrum of events to be held. Remember we are talking about ministry. Each one Reach one!

There is a school of thought that purports most Christians are "under-employed" within the church. Too many churches have formed an underdeveloped, underutilized labor pool within the membership and show limited results in reaching and building people. By tapping into this pool of people we grow not only ministry but also sow into the lives of the body, creating the opportunity for each one to reach a new level in the purpose for their own life.

The challenge with volunteers is not only with the volunteer, but the person who is responsible for placing that volunteer on a task. Before you can call upon "Sister Brown" to serve on a committee or in a specific area, it is helpful to understand her strengths and weaknesses.

Develop a survey to be taken by each person that wishes to volunteer for any ministry within the organization. It will allow you to get an idea of where they could be most beneficial on a project that may arise within the organization. Personality skills, Communication skills, Administrative skills, Technical skills, Design skills, Negotiation skills, Leadership skills.

Your survey could be simple asking a few questions like:

1. What are your current areas of involvement?

2. Which of these areas of current involvement do you enjoy and wish to continue? Are there any other areas that are of high interest to you?

3. Are there any changes in your ministry participation that you would like to now make?

4. Do you have any other comments, suggestions, questions or concerns?

Many times we lose volunteers because we use them to fill last minute holes that crop up without thought as to their usefulness in the slot. Volunteers are an integral and vitally important part of inclusion. Get out of the mindset that they are an afterthought or the last thought in the process. Include them in your plan from the beginning and solicit their input as early as possible. What you need them to do may not yet have arrived in the planning process but they have the ability to plan their time for service in advance. The vantage point they have is much closer to the ground and the feedback they receive will make the difference on many of the decisions you make going forward toward bettering your future attempts at like events.

Let's also take a quick look at the Leaders that work with our volunteers. There is a word that we use quite a bit, though I think its definition has become blurred and that word is **Delegation**.

Taking mounting tasks off of your plate and giving them to someone else for the sole purpose of getting them off your plate is not delegation. What this does is leave projects undone or allow for subpar completion. It can kill morale for a volunteer that feels as though the top is doing nothing other than piling work on the subordinates.

Delegation requires more than merely ridding oneself of a responsibility. In order to be effective the *delegator* must ensure that the *delegate* receives the following:

> **Known Expectations**: What is to be achieved by the completion of a certain task?

> **Core Knowledge**: If you are going to give a new task to someone make sure the appropriate training is provided as well as the exposure to

resources to aid in the success of mastering the new skill set.

*Resources*: Don't expect anyone to do a job without the very same tools you would expect to have access to.

*Accountability*: Make sure follow up and evaluation are provided for the person performing the task.

*Appreciation*: The acknowledgement that someone was able to accept more responsibility, complete a task and benefit the process is always in order.

## WORKING WITH CHILDREN AND YOUTH:

Events geared toward children and youth bring an added level of responsibility as you plan. Building in security for both the event participants and volunteers who are in this age range (5-17) as well as the attendees in the same age category is vital.

Risk management training should already be addressed within your organization as a standard practice. You as the ministry event manager must adhere to these same guidelines when executing an event so as to protect those involved and to limit the liability that may be incurred for failure to uphold these standards in the case of a problem.

Youth events are always lively and full of fun but they cannot be a free for all where unsupervised children are allowed to roam and fall prey to abduction or get into mischief. Channel their energy and utilize their talents in a productive way. Involve and engage them to do their part in working with *their* Pastor's vision and their church's mission.

Chaperones, properly trained in working with children are a must. A standardized operational procedure must be in place in case of an emergency. Again, this should already be in place within your church; however these procedures must be enacted without fail in *every* event produced involving young people.

Lastly there needs to be a clear understanding of your church's policies as it pertains to child abduction. Time is of the essence in these situations and time is only best utilized if people know what and what NOT to do in a specific situation.

## UTILIZING SPONSORSHIPS:

Funding events, especially large events, is a task that usually no one wants to handle. We look to what we view is the largest resource and that is normally the organization itself to fund events and write a check for all expenses. Unfortunately this is not always feasible nor should it be the norm. The use of sponsorships to underwrite the activities of ministries is a common practice but one you must get appropriately acquainted with fairly quickly.

Hopefully there is already in place, a procedure for writing and securing sponsorships. Your organization as a whole needs to be mindful of the resources that are available within your community and how often they are being tapped on behalf of the many various ministries of the church. Your church may approach a corporation with a substantial sponsorship request and receive a negative response because that same corporation has been tapped repeatedly for small amounts of money from various ministries in your church multiple times during the course of the year.

There should be one voice authoring the requests for

sponsorships. Templates should be available for request letters and a recording system to track which ministries are requesting what items from what companies.

Your first step with securing sponsorships is actually setting a realistic budget for your event and getting that budget approved. To throw out arbitrary numbers in the round thousands as sponsorship levels is not the best way to go. A smarter idea for mid sized events, is the use of the line item sponsorship. Have sponsors cover the costs of specific products and services that will be needed for the execution of that particular event.

Determine your needs and your budget will outline all of your expenditures. You should acquire quotes for the products or services you will require.

> *People,*
> *do business*
> *with*
> *People.*

Next review the current resources available within the congregation. Who within your congregation possesses the skill sets or  works for a company that may be able to provide these resources at a favorable rate?  Look to the vendors that the church currently uses for some of these services on an ongoing basis. Vendors that know you are much more willing to work with you because *"people do business with people"*. Working from a "line item" perspective will cover all of your bases, fund your projects and expand your relationship with your vendors.  They may also be the entre to additional vendors that can provide needed services.

Identifying people on your volunteer database that have experience in Business Development i.e. Sponsorship will make quick work of this piece of your project.  Having a group of people you can pull from to work on developing the levels of sponsorship and making contact with potential sponsors will free you up to continue moving the project forward.

## DETAILING THE DEBRIEF:

One key area that isn't always implemented in the execution of events is the follow up. We plan for a perfect event and spend endless hours of work to achieve that goal, but don't reflect on the actual outcome to see what went well and what didn't and why.

Problems are normally easy to fix once identified. Something went wrong and the reason we know it went wrong is because someone responded with opposition. That becomes easy to fix because we know what the objective was, where the problem occurred and can backtrack to where the genesis for the problem laid.

With some tweaking, this same problem should not reoccur. But what about what went right? Taking a look at things that went right to see if they can/should be implemented in other places is often key. If it worked right for Children's Day, could it work right for the Single's retreat?

Get feedback from every level of the process; including those that merely attended the event. What was the experience like for them?

We all have a great deal of enthusiasm for planning before the event, but follow-up needs to be an equal part of the process. While we don't enjoy criticism and given, it doesn't always come to us in the manner we can appreciate, it does hold many of the keys to hosting better future events for a specific audience.

**CHAPTER NINE**

# CREATING THE STANDARD

Getting to a place of standardization is going to take a bit of time to develop procedures that work globally for your organization. Once they are in place however, you will still experience both a learning curve and an acceptance curve.

Change is difficult for many people and during the change phase, it almost always seems easier and more efficient to go back to doing things the way they had been done in the past.

Reinforcing protocols and correcting lapses will help in ensuring that the new standardized procedures begin to engrain themselves into the fabric of your organization in the same way the old procedures once found a home.

Where do you need policies, protocols and procedures in your organization? What types of tools will you need to better implement and monitor the new procedures? We are going to speak to many of those answers in this chapter.

## THE EVENT MANAGEMENT PROCESS:

Already you have done a mountain of work and hopefully compiled a great deal of information on both the event tasked to you and the method through which events are executed at your organization.

You should by now have a clear understanding of both

the event, its history and your organization's objectives. Now you can really get the ball rolling with a clear cut plan of action. The event management process takes all the information you have compiled and allows you to interpret that information in order to plan for success. Once you have a clear cut plan, not only do you know where you're going and how you're going to get there, but everyone that works with you will also have a road map. Your plan is not meant to constrain, but to support.

*Project Management : 101*

- Define a clear vision and outcome
- Identify all parties involved
- Understand the needs of each of the key stakeholders
- Develop a plan that will nurse success
- Create an event flow plan identifying event partners
- Create an event timeline
- Create effective Plan B
- Identify the measurements for success
- Ensure clear communication
- Identify and mange risks associated with the event
- Take a team approach to achieving the outcome and ensure everyone has what they need to be successful.
- Debrief and follow up, post event to review successes and challenges.

## THE EVENT TIMELINE:

The timeline again is not a new phenomenon but it falls short in many cases due to its design. It is imperative to understand the timeline is not a linear prospective but rather a global overview.

So as not to blur lines I will refer to the *event timeline* as the checklist that will walk you through the process of planning an entire event. For the <u>day</u> of the event, rather than using the term *timeline*, we will refer to that document as a <u>*run sheet*</u>.

The basic event timeline skeleton for every event held by your organization will look the same. It can be stored as a template and disseminated to every ministry leader within the organization. The items on this skeleton are the baseline procedures observed within your organization. Items like submission of requests to hold an event, submission of event overview for approval, request of date etc...

This allows everyone to start off on the same foot and engrains the process as a check and balance so no one skirts the process. As you get into the specifics of an event the items included on the timeline will become more specific.

- Any Pre or Post activities
- Travel support
- Administrative Activities
- Documentation and License Approvals
- Preparation lead times
- Installation
- Predetermined deliverable dates

## TRACKING THE EVENT PROCESS:

The above referenced checklist should be able to track every task needed to be accomplished, who will do it, when will it start, how much should it cost and when it will be completed.

As well, it will allow you to keep an eye on your progress and how you are doing at meeting your goals in a timely, budgeted manner. This document will eventually serve as a terrific piece to share with your client at any point in the process and let them know how things are progressing and where they stand in regard to the budget. You may also be able to revisit how realistic your planning windows are if target dates are continually being missed.

## THE COMMUNICATION PLAN:

How is information being funneled to all of the stakeholders? We have taken several steps to identify the players, now how do we keep everyone in the loop throughout the planning process?

An *event overview* should be reviewed with your team.

*Design Boards,* also called *Inspiration Boards* ( Figure 3) are a visual aid that can serve to better and more clearly communicate the expected end result to people before it is actual completed. These boards can be created with swatches of fabric, images from publications, sketches and paint samples. Design boards may prove especially helpful for larger events. This item will give a visual of the end product. It will visually set the direction everyone is working toward.

Figure 3

*Event timeline* as mentioned previously, this is the global list of tasks to be completed for the project along with deadlines for the completion of each task and an assigned person accountable for the task.

*Event Run Sheet*—also mentioned earlier in this chapter, this document is shared with your team, all ministries and vendors to govern the smooth flow of the event day. It allows the structure of the event to be viewed from multiple perspectives and gives everyone involved with up to date information. This tool is a *strong guide* and not the rigid law. It allows those running the event to keep a gauge on where things are and to recover from unforeseen changes. Change is a reality. It's how you handle change that will speak to your success.

*Copy all contracts.*    These should be on file with your organization,   with the ability to be reviewed as the project progresses to ensure the project is in compliance. Understanding what your contracts provide for and what they don't provide for is critical. As well the contract holds you within a certain set of criteria that must be met. All contracts are two-way. You will give remuneration for a service and they will provide a service for remuneration.  If either side does not meet their obligation there are consequences that will be levied.

*Walkie-Talkies*: Identifying the right walkie talkie for your organization may take some trial and error.  Range, cost and quantity will all play a part in the model that is right for your needs. Rental units can be used for large events until your organization deems it necessary to cover the cost of purchasing a large number of units for the ministry.

*On site signage, maps, programs and personnel.*    This is your communication point with your audience. Whether they are designed and printed internally or externally, the message they convey must be creative and concise.

## PROJECT MANAGEMENT TOOLS:

One of the smartest ways to reach your desired goal is by using the correct tools.  With the correct tools you will be buoyed by organization and have the ability to share information and updates,  in a timely manner,  with all parties.

*Event management software* is recommended; however research a demo version before purchasing.  There are a number of manufacturers that have designed software specifically customized for use by churches and faith based organizations of all sizes. While others have found that solid contact management software can be customized to suit their needs.

*Scheduling software*: Scheduling of space is crucial. A standardized method for space requests should be put into place and adhered to by both ministry personnel and those from the outside requesting space, if this is something you allow.

Recurring groups can have space scheduled for a complete year, leaving the remaining open spaces to be used for spontaneously scheduled events or opened to the general public for an additional revenue stream. By having a standardized process you have the ability to review not only the space request but to look at the activities taking place globally in your space to avoid inappropriate overlap.

For instance, you would never want to schedule a wedding at the same time a band or choir rehearsal is taking place due to the sound carrying and disrupting the sanctity of the ceremony.

*Budget Manager:* This tool will track all budgeting and all expenditures. It will also keep track of when payments and balances are due and have been paid. It will also give a clear picture of where you are in regards to meeting your budget at any given time. This will of course not supersede your accounting department and is not meant to alter the way funds are handled or allocated within the organization; however an on paper accounting for the project will keep the project on task rather than your accounting department letting the Pastor know after the fact.

*Timeline Manager:*  Most event management software can be customized to generate both standardized event timelines and run sheets covering all the tasks that your organization requires.  Once designed these can quickly and automatically be generated for others to follow.

This is an important step in grooming others to lead events. Additional responsibility can be given to leaders in training while ensuring that the integrity of the event process will be maintained, as they will have set guidelines to follow.  As the organization grows it is very simple to make global changes to how ministry is executed by adding or removing certain tasks within the software to populate these lists going forward.

*Guest Manager:*  Are invitations being sent out to the event?  A guest manager can track responses, entrée selections, seating and room assignments for the entire event and even format escort and place cards.

Having the ability to generate lists pertaining to guests in a number of different ways is enormously helpful depending upon who is using the list.

> *Your greeters can sort the list by last name in order to direct guests quickly to their seats.*

> *Catering may choose to list them according to entrée selection to ensure their counts are accurate and expedite plating.*

> *Your floor director may list them by table or area to be able to quickly see where open seats lie in the case of a guest not on the list.*

> *You can list them by event if you have a weekend's worth of events scheduled or are running a conference with a number of breakout sessions.*

*You can sort out VIP's along with their adjutants to be ensured you have both proper seating available as well as parking reserved.*

*Seating software:* When designing floor plans and scaled room layouts, it is not good enough to "eyeball" where things will go, you need to know for sure how many tables or chairs will the room hold and how many people at each table or area. You must learn how to work around room obstructions (doors, windows, columns etc.) and know where power is located. Can you answer the question of "What size dance floor will fit?" Seating software will allow you manage all of this and can help you to identify where certain people need to placed within the room.

Dais seating, VIP tables, handicapped seating etc. If you have numbered seating as in a theatre, the seating software will assist in giving you a visual of how seats are filling and where you may have holes. It will help in the pricing of seating as well and being able to sell Premium Seating if this is something desired.

The basis for any event is a standardized method. However when ministry is involved additional, specific considerations must apply. You as a Ministry Event Manager (MEM) must be attuned primarily to the tenor of the event. For this reason your logistical plan and standardized operating procedures must be sound. The ability to manipulate YOUR plan to the BIGGER plan of what may be happening in ministry will rely on everyone knowing where they should be going and ready to change course at a moment's notice.

## DEFINING SPACE:

While we attend church services every Sunday, many, many churches are operational seven days a week for a variety of activities like school, classes, musician, choir and dance rehearsals, athletics, baptisms, prayer services, funerals, weddings, banquets and many other types of sessions.

How well do you know the spaces available in your buildings? Creating an inventory of available spaces along with their capacities in a variety of set ups is a solid start.

Can food be consumed in certain areas? Are instruments available in certain areas? Which spaces have audio and video capability. Knowing this information will help you to better allocate space and determine whether you can adequately accommodate an event or even several events concurrently.

Creating both pre-event and post event checklists will also ensure that your spaces are maintained at tip top shape and remain ready for both internal and external usage.

## MANAGING VENDORS:

The preparation you have done this far should gain you enough information to begin the process of vendor recommendation.

Now is not the time to begin looking for "a guy to do the job". Vendor relationship building is an ongoing part of the process and one that needs to be looked at periodically even with existing relationships.

Who is currently supplying the need? This may be as far as you need to go. Your organization may have someone in mind, whose work they like and trust and whose services are within budget or are already contracted.

Beware of merely using the same vendor solely because

they have always done the job.   This could be considered Old Testament thinking. If they are not up to par with the improvements you are making in the ministry or are too expensive based on the market adjusting itself due to new technologies, the opportunity for another vendor to better serve your organization may be at hand.

Be equally aware if someone is charging little of nothing and only giving you services that amount to little of nothing.   Renegotiating may help you   secure better services and strengthen an existing relationship.

## WHO IS THE RIGHT VENDOR?

A great vendor is a great vendor but may not be the BEST vendor in every situation.  Sometimes if you are working within a niche you will find one vendor's strengths are of particular interest to you and the specific project you are looking to execute.

The faith based community may often feel that a secular vendor may not have an appropriate respect or understanding of protocols and procedures observed while in the edifice. Issues like walking across a pulpit or trampling upon sacred areas when installing equipment or attire to be worn during a worship service are often areas of contention. Perhaps it's the observance of certain hours of the business day that may be hours of prayer or worship within your edifice.

The right vendor wants to understand your specific needs because they want to build a lasting relationship with you.  By your taking the time to work with a new vendor and bringing them up to speed on how things operate in your world, they can accommodate those needs and deliver the needed services all while making a show of great customer service.

## CRISIS:

Being aware of the crisis plan for your organization or at least aware of the person responsible for enacting it is an important step not everyone takes into consideration. Understanding how the actions you take  impact the evacuation of the building, or the locating of a lost or abducted child are crucial.

Equally important is understanding the chain of command for your building.  Who gets alerted in what type situation and in what order?  While the Pastor is eventually apprised of everything, He or She is not necessarily the first point of contact for every situation. Understanding the chain of command can not only save lives and expedite assistance it can also ensure that the proper steps are taken to keep the organization's liability intact.

## TAKING YOUR EVENTS OFFSITE:

The majority of your events will probably be housed within your own building or somewhere on the ministry's campus and occasionally you may venture off site and find that you may  be better suited by the lease of an outside location either to accommodate a larger number of people or to offer a different setting. These could include: Banquet halls, stadiums or arenas, theatres, playhouses, beaches, amusement parks, convention centers or museums.

Read all of the contractual fine print and make sure you understand it.  Ask the question "*How do the contract requirements fall in line with the items we have already determined in our planning?*" Are there any red flags? Be aware of service charges, food and beverage minimums and what items count toward that minimum. Deposit amounts, dates for guarantee counts and final payments. Read over the cancellation terms and the disposition of your deposit in the case of cancellation. Use of the loading docks and parking availability as well as the time allotted for set up and break down. Be sure to inquire as to whether the venue is a unionized establishment or not. A unionized establishment will require your  use of union workers for many of the tasks to be accomplished and these costs may be significantly higher than vendors of your own choosing, especially if your event takes place during a time when they must be paid a higher wage (this includes set up and break down. i.e. Set up for a sunrise service on a Sunday morning or breakdown after a Watch Night or New Year's Eve Service).

If anything peculiar sticks out to you, highlight the items and bring them to the attention of the person authorized to sign contracts within your organization,  along with your proposed solutions. Don't just hand over the contract and say "You're not going to like this...."

Once the terms have been agreed to and the contracts have been signed.  Be sure to transfer all pertinent contractual dates onto your event timeline to assure deadlines are met. This includes taking into account the lead time needed to have checks/payments processed within your organization.

I remember clearly the task of working with a large church that wanted to welcome in the new millennium by having their entire congregation worship together in one location.  The church's congregation at the time hovered in the five thousand range and they were accustomed to worshiping in three smaller services every Sunday.

The Pastor felt that it was important on this a once-in-a-lifetime occasion, to have everyone together in one service and to be able to accommodate those within the City that may feel as though the turn of the Millennium is their opportunity to give their life to Christ.

Now this is a large church with staff and multiple ministries of capable individuals. As we began the search for a space to hold this service we found that we needed to consider many more items than merely instructing the congregation and greater community of an alternate location.

We had our first major experience with Unions. We wanted to hold a service on a Friday night to begin after business hours and end at the stroke of midnight on Saturday morning. We quickly learned that the unions handled everything.  Audio, video, power, installation of risers... everything.  And we were at the mercy of their rate scale. All of our able bodied volunteers were now spectators in a large number of areas.

Late nights and weekends all equated to time-and-a-half for the union workers. This in addition to the fees that the venue charged for the space, concessions, break out rooms and dressing areas, onsite parking, insurance etc. etc. etc.

So back to the "budget" board we went.  We were able to successfully negotiate some of the fixed costs that were associated with the leasing of the space.  But there were also some things that we had to cut.  Fewer changing rooms, shorter time frames for sound checks. We encouraged members that served for the service to bring a snack  to save money on concessions and to use public transportation or carpool to reduce the number of parking spaces needed.

Creating a plan for the implementation of this event required a change in how we viewed what we were accustomed to handling, and working with a group of hired hands who were <u>all business</u>.  Our focus became transforming this venue that was used for everything under the sun every other day of the year into a sanctuary that encouraged people to worship and give their lives to Christ.

By refocusing the efforts of the ministries on hand, the space did indeed become a sanctuary that gave the congregation and the community a sure sense that they were indeed in God's House.  Many people gave their life to Christ that evening. This event set the stage for this church to begin producing larger scaled events over the coming years, events that number in the tens of thousands for attendance. They targeted many different groups, with a proficiency they had not possessed before. In turn their ministry grew, their membership grew and ultimately their message was sent forth further and further.

## BECOMING AN EXTERNAL VENUE:

You have become "*Master of your Domain*" let us take a 180° turn and look at the use of YOUR facility as an external venue whereby developing a new revenue stream for your organization.

Your organization can determine to what extent you would be comfortable leasing certain spaces, to whom and for what purposes.

If you currently have a licensed catering ministry you now also have an in-house caterer for all events requiring food service. If you have not already done so you will have to send all catering personnel through food service training and certification. Additionally you will have to have your food preparation areas inspected and given license to prepare and serve food. Once you have gotten through the certification processes required by your local city and state authorities you can begin to establish the standards that will be observed by those wishing to use your venue to host their event.

Being your own  in-house caterer creates another revenue stream for your organization. In addition to a leasing fee for space, you will be able to establish fees to provide all food service within the spaces leased by your organization.

You have the ability to establish food and beverage minimums. A food and beverage minimum defines the minimum amount of food and beverages a leaser must commit to purchasing for their event in order to lease the space. Why is this a good idea?  Let us think back about resources.  What does it cost your organization to lease space? The space must be cleaned. It must be monitored with a staff person for the duration of the event in case something were to go wrong.  There are costs associated with the heating and cooling of the space as well as the lights, everything has a cost that must be covered.  Is it worth it to incur those costs and potentially LOSE money? No, it is not. A food and beverage minimum will ensure that the events you cater will be worthwhile from a cost standpoint.

If full in-house catering is not an undertaking your organization is ready to undertake at this point in time you may also consider mandating beverage service only. Beverage service is an offering we are beginning to see more and more.  The venue does not offer food services but does mandate that all beverages and servers be secured through the venue at set pricing.  In addition beverages, which can simply consist of soft drinks, coffees and teas to more elaborate beverage offerings like mixed (nonalcoholic) signature drinks and sparkling cider.

You will need to design a contract to be signed by those leasing your space. It is advisable to have separate agreements for catering services and the leasing of space. Ensure that your contract outlines both the date and time span for the lease of space and covers set up time before the event and clean up time after the event. You will need to spell out each criterion within the contract to avoid any misunderstanding. It will be your task to define the scope of each area of the contract. Deposits and payment structure, late fees and penalties for lack of clean up and cancellation, insurance requirements from those leasing the space etc.

We spoke earlier of the need to have a working knowledge of the spaces that you currently have at your disposal. Once you are familiar with spaces like the Chapel, Sanctuary, conference room, classrooms, banquet hall, and other spaces that could be used for meetings or events, you will need to know their capacities in varying configurations. Further along in the book we will visit the different types of room set ups, how they differ and under what circumstances they are generally implemented.

There will be days and times that certain spaces will of course not be available for lease either due to your own church ministry events or because an outside event may coincide with an internally sponsored event and cause a conflict. You will work closely with the person dedicated to scheduling of spaces and perhaps implement a first right of refusal to all dates and spaces for internal church events over external events.

You will need however, to be able to keep your internal scheduling timely if you are going to get any benefit of having space open to external leasing. Your external clients will want to plan in advance as well. By encouraging internal ministries to plan out both their meetings and events a year out will give you a good idea of space and dates remaining available for external leasing.

Be aware that opening your facility to external leasing will invite a greater amount of wear and tear on the building and its furnishings. This will need to be taken into consideration when pricing to cover fees for the minor renovation, upkeep and the replacement of items due to ordinary wear and tear that will need to occur.

What will be included with the rental of space in your facility? Tables and chairs? Will you allow the use of your instruments for musically related events?

Parking spaces will need to be considered. Will they be included or excluded from the rental. Once you become "open for business" potential clients will want to utilize as much as they possibly can from your resource inventories. Having predetermined what will be available for public utilization will be important. Some items you may not want to have used by the general public. Shuttle busses and van may carry a large insurance liability if used for non church related events. Your Pastor may not want the church's pulpit furniture to be utilized by an outside congregation that is broadcasting its event. You must always keep in the forefront of your mind how anything utilized under your roof by an outside party could potentially have an adverse effect on your ministry.

What types of events do you want to be available to host? Perhaps you want to keep things small and open your leasing to members only for small social gatherings. Perhaps you are very well equipped technologically and only want to open your space to musical events and small corporate meetings? Others of you will want to go whole hog and  have your space utilized for banquets, plays, indoor and outdoor events. You call the shots just be consistent.

Understand from the outset that you will be saying No to a number of requests for various reasons. The space may be available but all of the other resources needed to execute an event are otherwise committed. Holy days may be off limit. This is to be expected and with time you will get into the flow of leasing space with ease.

## CAPTURING THE MOMENT:

Having an event documented is important whether to the host of the event or to the organization benefiting from the event. Having your own photographers to capture the event is vital. While outside media is always attractive, you cannot always rely on their availability to cover your event. But having your own photographers on site will allow you to follow up with both internal and external media sources, provide content from the event and have post coverage which is also vital. Not to mention a great source of GOOD images of your work for future clients to view.

*You possess the right of refusal. Determine the best way to say No, in advance.*

**CHAPTER TEN**

# EXPANDING YOUR REACH

Working in a niche industry such as the faith based community will fine tune some skills that make taking your expertise out into the greater secular community both possible and profitable.

Opportunities for planners that have a comprehensive grasp on the development and execution of large scale events are far ranging to include:

- Fundraisers
- Philanthropic Events
- Corporate retreats
- Annual Galas and Banquets
- Themed Parties Celebrations
- Family reunions
- Celebrity Fundraisers
- Sporting Events
- Book Signings
- Grand Openings
- Press Conferences

## "THONS": WALK-A-THON, READ-A-THON, MARATHONS:

A few of these areas, once you are outside the purview of a church, will require you to have at least a cursory knowledge of some project aspects normally handled by a given department within the organization. Knowing what you need, is half the battle to getting the assistance you need to accomplish the task. The arms and legs i.e. volunteers, may already be within the organization hosting the event and placed at your service or as you grow they may be in house services that you can offer for a fee.

We spoke very recently about sponsorship, be clear when working on an outside event like the ones listed above who will be responsible for this task.  If it is you, be sure you are prepared for the additional workload and that you have assistance that possesses this skill set.

## SECURITY:

Always have go-to security available.  They need not always be big burly men ready to throw someone through a window,  you really want someone with keen eyes whose sole job is to blend in and watch what is going on at the event and respond accordingly.

Also, always remember to include a female person on your security detail. Look into off duty police officers as well as specialized security providers if your event really requires a heightened level of attention.

## CELEBRITY APPEARANCES:

How do you handle celebrity, how do you handle their entourages and how do you handle the demands? First thing is simple, if you are star struck, look for another niche. This is not the time for photographs and autographs, this is business. Everyone wants to work with celebrities in order to get this type of experience on their resume and to be able to say "We've worked with so and so" but Be Prepared. Ensure you have the manpower needed to dedicate to a personality of their stature. Negotiate all details in advance and be prepared for changes either in schedules or in demands.

Most celebrities are scheduled very tightly if you are not on your P's and Q's your window of opportunity can elapse. Travel arrangements, plenty of ground transportation, holding areas and the use of likenesses need to be considered. Also be aware and cognizant of why you want to deal with a celebrity personality, if the demands become outrageous, are you willing to walk away from the business knowing that if you cater to unreasonable demands they may become the "norm". Keep your pride and dignity and go after Good Business even if no one knows their name but you and their bank.

## SWAG BAGS:

Such a hot trend, the swag bag. Where do you get donations for these bags?  Where do you even get the bags? Swag bags really need to be given some thought, there is nothing worse than a huge bag half filled with paper collateral materials from vendors. This is another great sponsorship benefit. If you can say to a potential donor that their item will be put in the hands of X number of people, there is a value to that.  Be specific in your requests to local vendors and make participation appealing in support of the event. Promotional items and samples have a cost to the vendor providing them; make the most of the swag bag for it to be an appealing option for vendor support.

## VALET:

Working with valet companies is another skill set you will need to learn to maneuver.  Where will the valet park the cars?  Side streets? A nearby garage?  If using a garage, what time do cars have to be out by?  How many cars will fit? Does the valet need a garage access key?  Do they have a pre-existing relationship with a garage? How many valets will you need and for how long, keeping in mind that you have a much heavier throng of cars at the beginning of the event than at the end, as people will leave an event at varying times. What will the valet wear? Yes, even something this detailed needs to be considered. Will the host pick up the tab for everyone or will the cost be split between the host and their guests? Will guests bear the full cost?

## STEP REPEAT:

If you do not know what this is, you need to. A step repeat is a custom backdrop that is used for publicity photos at an event. The images on the backdrop are usually of the sponsors of the event and are usually earned at a cost (hint: sponsorship opportunity) Placement of this item is crucial. It needs to be the first stop guest make upon entering into our event. Have a photographer dedicated to this area and an assistant with that photographer. The assistant will document the name of the person and the number of the image from the photographer.  Once the images come back to you from the photographer you will be able to easily identify each person in every picture. Where to get the piece designed and printed locally is a must know.  And have a backup printer just in case. Ask the questions, Consult your team. Figure it out!

## HONORARIUMS:

We do like to get things for free, but the saying "You get what you pay for." does hold true.

What is an honorarium?

> *A payment given to a professional person for services for which fees are not legally or traditionally required.*

If you are working with a speaker whose presence will greatly attract support of your event there should be an honorarium paid.   Speaker's fees for professional speakers can run into the tens and even hundreds of thousands of dollars per appearance.   Budget in an honorarium to show your appreciation for the speakers' presence.

*Remember,*

*You get*

*what*

*you pay for...*

**CHAPTER ELEVEN**

# THE PUBLIC EYE

The truth of the matter is that not everyone believes as you do. For this reason it is important to monitor how what your organization says and does is portrayed by the greater public. Everyone will have an opinion and that is fine as long as their opinion is formed from accurate information.

Hiring a public relations (PR) firm to oversee the media aspect of your event can be money well spent. Keep in mind however that it can be done internally as well by canvassing your congregation for public relations professionals willing to volunteer time and expertise. There should be one person on staff responsible for being the voice of the organization. This is the person that will proof all communication going out on behalf of the organization as well as communicating directly with the Pastor on specific speaking points.

Creating a comprehensive list of media contacts before an event is crucial. Research area publications, television and radio stations and identify the appropriate contact person to cover your type of event. One outlet may have several different people you will work with depending on the event and its purpose.

Develop a press release for your event and design a few pitches. A pitch is a direct communication to a writer, reporter, blogger or editor via email or telephone in an effort to persuade them to cover your news. Pitches are usually <u>brief</u> and offer information that is customized to the news outlet and editor.

But let us back up and get a clearer understanding of Public Relations, Marketing and Advertising. Often the terms are used interchangeably. That is pretty much an indication someone doesn't know what they are talking about. While they all work in conjunction with one another they are different.

Public Relations versus Advertising, what is the difference?

*Advertising you pay for, Publicity you pray for.*

Anonymous

Public relations or PR is a more cost-effective marketing tool than advertising, but it's only <u>part</u> of a complete marketing strategy. Public relations and advertising do the same function of <u>promoting</u> a brand but they are different in how they operate.

COST—As stated in the above quote, you are going to pay for advertising. Public relations differs in that you receive free media coverage.

CREATIVITY —Through advertising you have the ability to design an ad of your choosing using your choice of representations. Public relations differs in that your message is completely in the hand of media outlet, they will decide how to present your information.

Advertising generates traceable returns in the form of sales, while public relations bring intangible benefits that give you results over the long term.

We are not really dealing with branding in our field as most of our events are isolated. The branding aspect would come internally from the organization. However the aspect of both advertising and PR that we are looking for revolves primarily around attendance and coverage.

For our purposes Advertising will probably generate ticket sales. Radio, television, outdoor (also known as billboard) even magazines and newspapers. These paid outlets will run your designed creative; their readers or listeners will see or hear it and hopefully respond by contacting you or the appropriate designee to purchase tickets. This generates money for you, although you will also have some sort of outlay of money or barter.

Through public relations we are looking for *coverage* on television, radio, magazine, newspaper, blogs etc. Your press release will hopefully spur these outlets to attend the event and write about the event, the organization and the cause. They will then get this content out before or after the event bringing recognition to your organization.

The other factor that differentiates advertisement and public relations is how people perceive each of them. When people read an ad in the paper they know that it is meant to sell a product or service while with public relations, when they read a third party account they tend to believe it more and they perceive it as an unbiased account. It is in these ways public relations generates more faith of the people, in your product, service or message in comparison to advertisement, which is taken by people as marketing or a gimmick.

## WRITING A PRESS RELEASE:

Is your news "news*worthy*?" The purpose of a press release is to inform the world of your news item. A good press release answers all of the "W" questions (who, what, where, when and why), providing the media with useful information about your organization or event. If your press release reads like an advertisement, reformat your message.

Start strong. Your headline and first paragraph should tell the story. The rest of your press release should provide the detail.

Write with the media in mind. Try to develop a story as you would like to have it told. Even if your news is not reprinted verbatim, it may provide an acceptable amount of exposure.

Tell the truth, the whole truth and nothing but the truth. Avoid fluff, embellishments and exaggerations. .

What is your angle? Try to make your press release timely. Tie your news to current events or social issues if possible. Make sure that your story has a good news hook.

You have a voice, use the right one.  Always use active rather than passive voice when writing. Verbs in the active voice bring your press release to life. Writing in this manner, helps guarantee that your press release will be read.

Keep it concise. Use only enough words to tell your story. Avoid using unnecessary adjectives, flowery language, or redundant expressions such. If you can tell your story with fewer words, do it. Wordiness distracts from your story. Keep it concise. Make each word count.

Speak English, Not Church. While a limited amount of jargon will be required if your goal is to optimize your news release for online search engines, the best way to communicate your news is to speak plainly, using ordinary language. Members of the faith based community use churchy jargon without really realizing it. Jargon is language specific to certain professions or groups and is not normally appropriate for general readership.

Avoid the hype. The exclamation point (!) is your enemy.

Get Permission. Companies are very protective about their reputation. Be sure that you have written permission before including information or quotes from employees or affiliates of other companies or organizations. It should not need to be said that everything going out for public consumption should be approved by the representative of your organization tasked with this responsibility. Any dispute resolution will favor the other company.

About your organization. Your press release should end with a short paragraph (a company boilerplate) that describes your company, products, service and a short company history. If you are filing a joint press release, include a boilerplate for both companies.

## FORMATTING YOUR PRESS RELEASE:

How you present your news is just as important as its content.

Mixed case. NEVER SUBMIT A PRESS RELEASE IN ALL UPPER CASE LETTERS. This is very bad form. Use mixed case.

Correct grammar usage. Always follow rules of grammar and style. If you are not familiar with the rules of writing style take some time and look into AP style and learn the rules associated with this style of writing.

Use a computer: Type your press release in a word processing software like Microsoft Word instead of composing online in a comment box. Take the time to do it right. Write, print, proofread. Rewrite, edit.

No HTML. Never embed HTML in your press release.

More than one paragraph. It is nearly impossible to tell

your story in a few sentences. If you do not have more than a few sentences, chances are you do not have a newsworthy item.

**CHAPTER TWELVE**

# Getting Down
# The Aisle

## THE MINISTRY OF WEDDINGS:

Churches large and small do have something in common when it comes to weddings. No matter the size of the church, the desire of a bride and her intended for a beautiful, memorable wedding ceremony is a unifying thread. More than 80% of today's weddings in the United States occur in churches or synagogues. How are wedding ceremonies approached in your church?

Many factors will play into whether weddings are handled by one person or may require the assembly of an entire ministry to ensure each and every ceremony is conducted without a hitch. Regardless of the approach there are certain standard operating procedures that need to be taken into consideration for the execution of every wedding ceremony conducted at your location.

*How many weddings take place at your location annually?*

*Are your wedding ceremony facilities available to the general public or member congregants only?*

*How liberal are the rules of the church as they pertain to weddings?*

*Are church musicians required to be used for wedding ceremonies?*

*How many locations are available for wedding ceremonies at your location?*

*How many ceremonies can take place simultaneously at your location?*

*How many people are capable of performing wedding ceremonies at your location?*

The answers to all of these questions will help to determine if your location is in need of a Wedding Ministry or if wedding ceremonies can be adequately managed by one or two  people. Keep in mind as well, that a wedding ministry may also be a wonderful opportunity for outreach to a demographic of your organization's membership that may have a love for this area.

## STARTING A WEDDING MINISTRY:

Upon the agreement that the need for a wedding ministry does exist and the proper approvals have been given to proceed, let us look at what you will need to consider;

Again we are going to start with your Pastor, how does the head of your flock approach wedding ceremonies?

- *Does he/she personally counsel all engaged couples?*

- *Does he/she personally attend the wedding rehearsal?*

- *Does he/she officiate at all weddings held at your location?*

Ideally, wedding ceremonies will be conducted at your organization with the primary objective being that the couple understands God's vision for marriage and that they are indeed aware of both the accountability and responsibility they are entering into once in covenant with God. To this end, your Pastor may have very strong feelings about how wedding ceremonies are conducted at your organization.

Once his/her thoughts are understood the wedding ceremony can be standardized. A basic order of service can be created for wedding ceremonies at your organization; this can then be disseminated to every couple during the wedding planning process to allow them to plan within the parameters that have been set by your organization.

# SAMPLE ORDER OF SERVICE

*Prelude selections*

*Entrance of Grandparents*

*Entrance of Parents of the Groom*

*Entrance of Mother of the Bride*

*Scripture Reading*

*Solo Selection*

*Entrance of Officiant, Groom and Best Man*

*Processional*

*Bridal Introit*

*Marriage Ceremony*

*Charge to the Couple*
*Exchange of Vows*
*Exchange of Rings*

*Solo Selection or Reading*

*Lighting of Unity Candle*

*Expression of Love to Parents*

*Pronouncement*

*Benediction*

*Recessional*

The order of service used at your location will be dependent upon a number of factors. If we look at the above sample ceremony layout we know that the following questions will need to be addressed as you begin to lay the foundation for your Wedding Ministry.

## MUSIC:

The first item we come across is music. Who will be responsible for providing music for wedding ceremonies? Will there be a set fee for musicians at every wedding? When will this fee be collected? Who is responsible for collecting this fee and making sure the musician is compensated? Will outside musicians be allowed to use the instruments at your location? Will couples have the opportunity to meet with musicians and determine what music selections will occur at their ceremony? How are soloists handled? Will the musicians provide soloist recommendations? Will couples be allowed to choose soloists who may not be members of your congregation?

## ATTIRE:

Does the church have modesty requirements for attire? Must all female members of the bridal party wear dresses? Should shoulders be covered?

Are scripture readings required? Do readers need to be members of the church or baptized in order to participate in the ceremony?

Is there a limit on the size of the wedding party?

Living in a society where the social mores have changed considerably over the past decades, we need to take a look at many of the ways people are living and see how that falls in line with the belief of your organization. For instance: Will there be a requirement that all attendants on the bride's side must be female and all attendants on the groom's side be male? If there is a female standing on the Groom's side will she be allowed to wear a tuxedo with pants or should she be in a dress? These are the types of questions that need to be pondered. By all means stay true to the beliefs of your organization, but be prepared for many requests to come that fall outside o those beliefs.

Will candle lightings, sand ceremonies and other types of personalization be allowed during the wedding ceremony? What about libation ceremonies?

Will the use of fresh flowers be permitted throughout the space? What about the dropping of petals on the aisle?

Will Communion be able to be served at wedding ceremonies? Will it be served to just the couple or for all attendees at the ceremony?

During what time frames and days of the week will wedding ceremonies be performed? Are there any months of the year when weddings will not be performed at your location?

Will there be any items provided to the couple for every wedding ceremony? Perhaps the organization will provide aisle runners or guest books for couples getting married.

Where will the bride be held awaiting her entrance? Will she be able to dress onsite or need to arrive completely ready?

Is there an inconspicuous entrance to receive the bride, away from peering eyes?

What type of pre-marital counseling will be required for weddings to occur at your location?

Will your location allow outside vendors such as florists

or lighting companies or specialty musicians such as harpists or quartets to set up at your location? Will you require liability insurance prior to them being allowed to operate on the premises?

Will you create and maintain a list of exclusive vendors for couples to choose from?

What will the limitations be for photographers and videographers during the ceremony?

Will the church's audio and video equipment be available for use by the couple for their wedding ceremony? Are there any additional fees?

When and where will vendors be allowed to deliver and set up?

Will you require couples to provide a copy of their wedding invitation and wedding program prior to printing to ensure it adheres to the protocols you have been put in place?

Will you have capacity criteria for ceremonies to be held in certain spaces? There is no sense in holding a wedding ceremony for 75 people in a 3000 seat sanctuary when there is a perfectly charming 300 seat chapel available as well.

Once you get answers to these questions and the others they will undoubtedly spark, create a document that can be given to everyone considering a ceremony at your location. Make sure the document is available as a .PDF file so that it can easily be emailed to couples. If your church has a website, consider posting as much information as possible on the website. This is often the first place people will look. This is a must if you plan on allowing non-members to use your facility.

Each member of your wedding ministry should be clear

on the policies and protocols of your church. You will need to determine how many people will serve on each wedding and what roles you need to have filled.

Who will be in contact with the Officiant to alert him/her that everyone has arrived and are ready to start the ceremony.

Who will ensure the marriage license is received, signed and returned to the couple?

Who will pin boutonnières and distribute flowers to the bridal party?

Who will ensure the sanctuary or chapel area is prepared and seats are reserved for family members?

Who will line up the bridal party?

Who will ensure musicians; readers and the Officiant have a program prior to the start of the ceremony?

Who will cue musicians for the change of music?

Who will handle the receiving line?

Who will meet the bride and escort her to a holding area?

Who will handle the seating of late guests?

Keep in mind the approximate number of weddings held annually at your location. It does not make sense to have a large wedding ministry of volunteers and only a small number of weddings annually. Too many people serving will actually distract from the event.

Setting ministry meetings to walk through mock weddings will prove very helpful. As you know or will find, once the wedding ceremony begins it is a very fast paced journey. Your entire team needs to be able to move quickly and efficiently while anticipating the next thing that will happen.

Another significant discussion item should be how you will interact with outside wedding planners. Will you communicate with a planner or only directly with the couple? Will you allow the planner and their staff to participate in the ceremony or will they only be spectators?

Also keep in mind that you will need to develop a debriefing process. What went well, that did not go well for EACH wedding. These debriefings will assist in your tweaking the protocols you wish to have upheld. I know of a church that will collect a "late start" deposit at the time the ceremony time and date are reserved to serve as an "incentive" for the wedding ceremony  to begin on time. Wedding ceremonies starting more than thirty minutes past the time of their reservation will forfeit the deposit. This suggestion came about in a debriefing session. Musicians, soloists and the Officiants all agreed that  a pattern of late starting weddings was developing and it was impacting their collective ability to keep other appointments and commitments. This debriefing allowed all involved parties to discuss options for solution taking everyone's input into consideration.

## Chapter Thirteen

# Weddings On Your Own

Much of this chapter will pertain to those of you interested in taking the leap into planning weddings on your own. I get so many questions about how to get into this field and I truly believe that you need to have a five star approach to working in the field of weddings whether it be internally for a ministry or church or from the standpoint of owning a practice that executes weddings professionally.

## Contracts/Agreements:

Let's just jump right into it. You need a contract. A contract signed by both parties that clearly outlines the duties to be performed, at what price and by when they shall be delivered. Stop dealing verbally. Stop *assuming* you were only going to do this or that or that the client meant this or that. Get it writing, get it signed and get to work.

What needs to be in your contract varies by state so make sure you have your contract reviewed by an attorney for validity.  It's all you have to fall back on in case of a dispute.  Outrageous claims or penalties are not necessarily legal even if signed off on in an agreement so you need to understand what the law allows in your area. Understand how long it will take to ratify a contract in your state.  Meaning how long does the client have after signing a contract to change their mind and be refunded their deposit.

What makes a contract? *a contract is an exchange of promises with specific legal remedies for breach.* Your contract needs to have the day and date of agreement and the day, date and time of the event in discussion and must be signed by both parties.

Be clear in the list of services that will be provided. Is it reception décor or *oversight* of reception décor? Two very different expectations. Length of services (unlimited consultations? 8 hours on the day of wedding? 3 vendor visits?), alternative services in case of a problem, last date to make changes or to provide final information needed to execute the contract.

Amount of deposit to be paid, payment schedule, overtime rates, if applicable, cancellation policy, name of contact person and the client's name and contact information. If changes need to be made or additional/ alternate terms are applicable they need to be initialed by all parties.

Utilizing the same processes and tools we have already outlined for ministry events is the foundation for the planning of any event. You, as a planner must have your back office and standard operating procedures in place **BEFORE** you start.

Please understand the business will be there. Take the time you need to get everything required together in a manner fit for public consumption. Nothing will derail business more than your putting forth an unorganized effort. The main reason a client, especially a bride is going to hire you is their ability to trust that you can competently handle this most precious event for them. If you do not have yourself together why will they trust you will their dream?

## ETIQUETTE: What is it?

*King Louis XIV's gardener at Versailles, perhaps famed Andre Le Notre or one of his subordinates, was faced with a serious problem: he could not stop members of the nobility from trampling about in the delicate areas of the King's garden. He finally attempted to dissuade their unwanted behavior by posting signs, called etiquets, which warned them to "Keep off the Grass." When this course of action failed, the King himself had to issue an official decree that no one could go beyond the bounds of the signs. Later, the name "etiquette" was given to a ticket for court functions that included rules regarding where to stand and what to do.*

Etiquette has become known as a term to dictate all the rules for courteous behavior, impeccable manners, dignity and civility.

The rules of etiquette are not merely guidelines you will find in various etiquette manuals and handbooks but as well the acceptable practices you will find at every location you find yourself hosting an event. Small things like genuflecting at an altar or not walking across a church's pulpit area are all items of etiquette for specific locations.

As a planner use good judgment. Do not assume what worked in one location will necessarily apply in the next location. Know the rules before you stray from them and give your client the pros and the cons of any decision they may make.

My favorite example:

A client wants to print invitations stating the ceremony will start an hour earlier than it is actually scheduled to begin, citing the fact that her family and friends are *"always late"*.

My feelings are quite clear. You are inviting family and friends who care about you and are <u>adults</u>. Why on Earth should they not be trusted to make it to your ceremony at the appointed time.  And more importantly why would you penalize those guests that are going to do the right thing and arrive on time for your stated, albeit fraudulent, start time and have to wait an extra hour because they were on time?  You make concessions for those exhibiting bad behavior and penalize those who do what is required.

Think about it.

## THE EMERGENCY KIT: Will Yours Curb an Emergency?

The first item every planner seems to get it a clipboard?  I find it hilarious because I have never been able to do anything constructive with a clipboard in my hand and secondly it is a red flag for everyone with a question or concern to inundate you with items to take you off track.

What is helpful is an emergency kit that can actually handle the emergencies that you will find yourself encountering.

## WHAT GOES IN THE KIT?

Antacids

Antihistamine (cold medicine)

Aspirin and non aspirin pain reliever

Band-Aids

Smelling Salts

Ice packs

Corsage pins

Writing pens

Sharpies markers

A roll of quarters

Cough drops

Mints

Sugar free hard candy

Pepto Bismol,

Feminine products

Sunscreen

Hairspray

Hand sanitizer

Brush and Comb

Barrettes

Hair and Bobby pins,

Lotion,

Hand (baby) wipes

Tissues,

Clear nail polish & remover

Baby powder

Toothbrush and paste

Spare garter in blue

Thumbtacks

Earring backs,

Safety pins (regular and extra large, heavy duty)

Masking tape

Sewing kit

Flashlight

Straws

Double sided tape

Double sided Velcro

Lighters

Buttons

Inexpensive cufflink set

Liken your thinking to that of McGyver. Everything in your kit has multiple duties. You can create/stabilize an intricate bustle with extra large safety pins, make a boutonnière with masking tape and a few altar flowers and lay an aisle runner with double sided Velcro.

Be careful when providing any type of medicine to individuals. It is not a bad idea to have a short release form removing yourself from liability to an adverse reaction to medication you give to an individual. Something seemingly minor like Tylenol versus aspirin can cause a problem.

## MAYHEM AND FOOLISHNESS:

The best laid plans should always take into account the reality that life will interrupt and throw you a curve ball. It is not the curve ball that derails your event or your reputation, it is how you handle the curve ball that will seal your fate.


Are you the Go To person or are you the buck passer.

# UNDERSTAND THIS; IT'S **ALL** YOUR JOB!

What do I mean? I mean working to solve a situation falls on your shoulder, regardless of where the genesis of the problem may lie.

Now, many times I have mentioned Stay In Your Lane. That still holds true. This is NOT the time to become bossy and tell people what to do.

You + Your Vendors (should) = TEAM.

They hold a vast amount of expertise and additional resources which you need to have access to. Making an enemy right now does not solve your problem.

Forget about whose fault it is and

# SOLVE. THE. PROBLEM.

What would **you** do?

*Photographer arrives to take pictures of the groom, who realizes that there is no shirt in his tuxedo bag. What to do?*

*Bride absolutely HATES her bridal bouquet and refuses to carry it or get dressed until it is fixed. What to do?*

*Unexpected family member shows up and feels as though, the couple would want him/her to have a flower for their lapel. What to do?*

*The videographer shows up with enormous lamps and hoods and tons of equipment and needs to set up but will be extremely obtrusive. What to do?*

*Bride forgets her veil. What to do?*

These are just the tip of the iceberg. Everything is possible at a wedding. You need to know what you're going to do in a given situation even if you have never experienced that situation before. Sounds crazy right? Well think about it this way, even if you have not experienced a specific situation most things happen in a way similar to something you HAVE already experienced. Is it a timing issue? Can you rearrange the events that will happen later to make up time or move some things around? Is it a materials issue? Can you make a call and send an assistant to acquire the resource while keeping everything else moving forward? Do you know your client well enough to work with their personality, sometimes it takes a soft touch sometimes it takes a sterner touch to move things along. And honestly, some things you will have to merely move past and count it as a mistake.

## THE COMPETITION:

I encourage everyone to get out of the mindset of competition right now. Perhaps it is not a realistic hope but I honestly believe that too much attention is put on beating out the other guy or winning the contract and not nearly enough attention is put on delivering five star services to each and every client.

Not enough attention given to refining and honing business practices to elevate the services that are offered.

Those two things alone will allow you to arise to the top of the pack  and to a position where you will not have to focus on who else is doing what, for you will be focused on which of the people ringing your phone will you be able to accept.

Having said that you do need to know what vendors and services are out there.  New businesses and established businesses will develop your network and give you options for types and levels of services as well as having backups and resources in times of trouble. Know what vendors are charging, what their fortes are, what their personalities are like.

Marketing yourself is important.  Do not take it lightly. Dedicate time and create a plan to maintain focus on your brand. You will never be able to dedicate enough time or resource this area of your business. I feel like I need to say it again.

Marketing yourself is important.  Do not take it lightly.

- Create a Facebook Fan Page and update it REGULARLY with information and images of your work. Create a  forum for dialogue either with brides or with other vendors.
- Get to know Twitter, and other social networking forums such as Plaxo and Linked In.
- Start and maintain a blog.  Your voice and your platform. Keep it updated regularly.
- Let people know you are doing this formerly. Notify your church and the local schools.
- Volunteer to plan a local event gratis as a way to network.
- Join a charity and establish yourself with a name/brand that is already established in the community.
- Sponsor a local sports team.
- Attend a bridal show as a vendor.
- Network with other vendors, as simple as setting an appt to meet or attending a meet and greet.
- Partner with an unlike vendor on a project.
- Create a direct mail program for area brides and vendors.
- Host a themed dinner party once a quarter so that the public can see your capabilities.

## PROFESSIONALISM:

Formally establish yourself as an industry professional. Get a professional email address.  Create a formal website presence.  Get your business license and have a dedicated phone line for clients to access your services.

Cutiepatooty992@aol.com is not a professional email address.

Having your 8 year old answer your business phone is not professional.

Long gone are the days when you have to have printed letterhead and envelopes which can be expensive, this allows you to spend a little more on an eye-catching business card, that will leave an impression.

If you will not have a commercial office it is wise to look into using a post office box or virtual office to avoid having your private residence address listed publicly, if you do not want clients "dropping by".

## WORKING WITH CLIENTS:

### THE COUPLE:

This is where it all begins. The couple. Not the bride but the couple. How does your consultation flow? Where does it take place?

The best suggestion I can make to you is not to view this as a sales pitch.

First understand yourself. What is your style? What kinds of personalities do you work best with? You need to interview every couple as closely as they are interviewing you.

If you know micro-managers rub you the wrong way, then look for those characteristics in the couple during the consultation. If people who can not make a decision drive you crazy look for those tendencies. If the bride really wants to plan her own wedding but everyone is telling her to get a planner, suggest a package that meets that need. You have to look for these things.

STOP TALKING.

LISTEN.

Introduce yourself and let the couple talk. You just shut up, take a few notes and LISTEN. Watch how they interact with each other? Does she have him speak at all? Does she look over to him for confirmation after every statement? Does he dictate the entire conversation? What is it they want? Do they know? Did they bring anything to show you what they like? Did they bring TOO much and they just like the idea of "having a planner".

You need to be able to look for clues and get an understanding of the people you are going to be spending a great deal of time with. They have already researched you on the Internet, gone to your website, called someone that used you for another event and gotten the skinny on you, so for you to give a sales pitch is unwarranted. If they have specific concerns, they will ask you outright. Once you have gotten an idea of what they are looking for, you need to broach the budget question. **YES**, right there at the consultation. Does all you have heard about what they want and envision match up with what they are trying to spend?

Additionally you need to get a feel for the *availability* of these funds. It's great to have a number in mind but are those funds available for use immediately as you begin to view venues and meet with vendors?

Couples will often "plan" to save the money they need for their wedding while they are planning. This strategy does not always work so well. A vendor available today is not necessarily a vendor available tomorrow. Unless your client is ready to sign on the dotted line and secure that service, you run the risk of losing out both on a specific vendor and/or specific pricing.

Now I must pause here because this is where so many planners go wrong. They get the question:

"How much does a wedding in _____ cost?"

If you try to answer this by providing a dollar amount you are a fool. A wedding costs exactly what a couple spends on it and not a cent more. Can someone host a wedding for more or less than a "national average"? Of course they can if they are willing to be flexible with certain items.

## THIS IS WHERE YOU START TALKING!!

Are they willing to reduce the guest list? Alter the time of day? Change the style of food service? Forego certain services? Or implement any other cost savings options? If the answer is "Absolutely Not! We must have all of these things." My suggestion to you is to offer them the name of a referral and decline the business. This couple will bring you grief, expecting you to do the impossible. Now if you are indeed a magician, by all means take the business and have a wonderful year of arguing, unmet expectations, tears and frustration toward a couple that will not listen to you. Expect to call in unimaginable favors from your vendors, family and friends and expect to lose money on this one. But hey, at least you will probably learn from the mistake and never take a client with the same red flags again.

### THE BRIDAL PARTY:

Now here is a touchy subject. The bridal party. Originally the bridal party had very specific duties and their assistance was vital. However many things have happened in subsequent years. More and more brides and her friends are living, not at their childhood homes, but in various states around the country due to post graduate studies and employment duties. Bridesmaids and Honor Attendants are no longer living around the corner but indeed around the globe. With taxing careers and great distances often involved the ability for bridesmaids to be as hands-on as a bride might like becomes difficult. Your role as a planner in many instances picks up where some of the bridesmaids roles leave off. But be careful to be respectful and mindful of their roles and assist the bride in redefining what each bridesmaid will be responsible for, even if it's just one task.

*A wedding costs exactly what the couple spends on it, not a dime more.*

PARENTS:

One of the greatest hinge pins in working with weddings comes with how you handle the couple's family members. Often this, not the opulent ceremony and reception, are the key to getting rave reviews and referrals.

You need to work smart and understand; "Everybody wants to be heard" and quite frankly at this joyous moment it is your job to *listen* to everyone. Now note, I said "listen" to everyone, not react and obey. The bride is your client and her mother may or may not be paying. Having a mother that feels as though she is on the outside looking in to her daughter's wedding is a set up for failure. But by honestly listening to a parent's thoughts, you can assure that they are a part of the process and an active participant. If she and her daughter don't agree that's not your problem. In many cases, by your taking the time to flush out how viable a third party's idea is or is not, will ultimately make your job easier. By merely taking the time to walk through ideas everyone can see how things will work together or how that idea may not be feasible with the plans already made. In many cases a Mom may see that the things she dreamed for her daughter 20 years ago, do not fit in with the themes of today's wedding.

## WHERE DO YOU START?

Planners can not wait to get their hands into the design of a wedding. You have a bride with all of these ideas and it is a fresh and new project and everything is great.

Hold your horses and curb your enthusiasm.

Rein it all in and before you look at a color swatch or cut outs from a magazine let us talk dollars.

Budget is absolutely the first conversation had with a new client.

How much? Where is it coming from? And what is it expected to cover. If they do not know, are not sure or just look at each other, there is work to do.

Very often I will get phrases like "My parents are going to help out." Or "My mom will chip in wherever needed." Or "My grandmother is going to give us something."

Not good enough. Send the couple off to speak with Mom, Dad, Grandmom and their banker to get a solid grasp on where funds are coming from in order to minimize surprises at the 11th hour.

If someone is paying for the dress, are they paying for the dress, the alterations, the veil and tiara undergarments and shoes? This is what we need to know and if they can not answer you they have not had the conversation with the person providing the money either.

Develop a budget based on the amount of money anticipated and have a frank conversation with the couple on the feasibility of that budget. Discuss options, must have items, and less important items.

Recalculate the budget to something that is feasible and have your client sign off on the budget. This makes clearing up disagreements in the future much easier. Your conversation would sound something like this:

*"We agreed you were spending ___dollars on flowers. The arrangements you have requested from the florist exceed that amount. Has the budget for this changed? Are you willing to reduce the amount of money you are allocating to something else in order to cover the costs of the flowers you have chosen?"*

Once money is out of the way, you can then actively begin further planning.

This is a sample budget structure.

Depending on where you are geographically in the country, the percentages are going to fluctuate a bit based on the market.

- Wedding and Engagement Rings (15%)
- Bride's Attire (head to toe inc. alterations) (5%)
- Reception (Site and Catering) (35%)
- Photographer/Videographer (10%)
- Music (Ceremony and Reception) (4%)
- Printing (Invitations etc. ) (4%)
- Flowers (10%)
- Wedding Cake (3%)
- Wedding Party Gifts (2%)
- Rehearsal Dinner (2%)
- Officiant (1%)
- Lighting (3%)
- Transportation (2%)
- Groom's Tuxedo (1%)
- Pre-Wedding Parties (3%)

A budget of $30,000 turns into this:

- Wedding and Engagement Rings ($4500)
- Bride's Attire (head to toe inc. alterations) ($1500)
- Reception (Site and Catering) ($10,500)
- Photographer/Videographer ($3000)
- Music (Ceremony and Reception) ($2800)
- Printing (Invitations etc. ) ($2800)
- Flowers ($3000)
- Wedding Cake ($900)
- Wedding Party Gifts ($600)
- Rehearsal Dinner ($600)
- Officiant ($300)
- Lighting ($900)
- Transportation ($600)
- Groom's Tuxedo ($300)
- Pre-Wedding Parties ($900)

I also always add in 5% as a miscellaneous number from their budget. Best case scenario it keeps them from going over as there are a few dollars on hold or if they stay on budget, they actually save money. The other thing I strongly recommend is to account for sales tax and service charges associated with the reception in the budget. These costs can easily mount to 20-25% of the cost of the reception budget which is a material amount over and above the budgeted number.

BUT WAIT ....

We are still not at the design phase. I know and understand you are chomping at the bit to look at fabric swatches but not yet.

If we assume that the date is agreed upon and we have looked at all contingency dates that work for the couple let us look at venues.

Why venues and not the design of the event? Well because the venue will greatly impact the design of the event. Spaces lend themselves to a certain feel. If your client has a definitive idea for the feel they are looking for that is great. However, I have seen far too many couples, say they want one thing and fall in love with something completely different.

If a religious ceremony is desired. The place of worship is your first stop. It is really not a situation of which comes first ceremony or reception. Ceremony comes first and the deference goes to the place of worship.

Is membership required? Are premarital classes required? Do they allow interfaith marriages? What is the churches policy for photography and videography? Are there décor restrictions, specifically flowers and the use of candles.?

Tread lightly with the church. Keep in mind the beauty of the event is not what is paramount in their mind. As you know from having worked internally with a faith based organization, the wedding ceremony is a very serious rite within the church. The church is concerned about the relationship being lasting and loving and a safe haven for all parties including the children that may come from the union. The focus for the church is the understanding of this and the intention of the couple to stay committed to each other.

Get a confirmation of the wedding ceremony location and time and then move forward to searching for a reception venue.

Do not show your client what they can not afford unless it is absolutely a last option and they have agreed to cut back somewhere else specifically because venue is their highest priority. Ask them to change their date before you show them something they can't afford.

Do not show them anything too small for their anticipated guest list.

Do not show them a venue not available on any of their proposed dates.

Make sure you do your due diligence by calling to verify rates for the year the event will take place, inquiring about any anticipated renovations, what is included in the rental cost, in-house vs. outside caterers and capacity for the type of reception you are planning.

PLEASE understand what the differences calculating capacity:

*Banquet seating* (with dancing vs. without dancing): This is traditional seating at tables of 8-10. Each guest has a seat at a table.

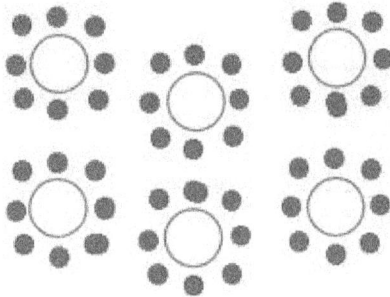

*Cocktail or Reception* style: This type of seating has limited seating and it is expected that guests will walk around and mingle, rather than be seated at a table.

*Theatre* style seating: This type of seating does not account for tables. This type of seating is primarily for ceremonies rather than receptions.

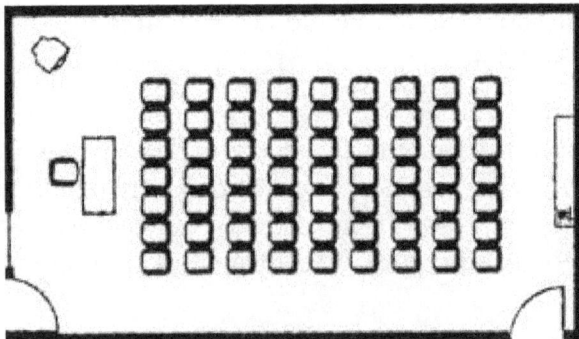

Once you have a list of venues that are available on their proposed date(s), within their budget and with adequate capacity you are ready to do a few venue visits.

I find it helpful to send the client a list along with website links to pictures of the venues so they can decide which venues they will want to visit.

Schedule a day of venue visits. It is much easier for a couple to compare apples to apples if the spaces they are seeing are fresh in their memory.

What do you do when the couple wants both the ceremony and reception at the same location?

This can be an ideal situation but it still require some thought and the asking of a few questions.

How long is the cocktail hour, this becomes the amount of time you have to *flip* a room. This is a perfect example of why we don't do design beforehand. If you are given an hour or less to flip your room, it may alter the design choices you make. It may require the need for additional laborers which will increase cost, taking up more of your budget.

What are the photo opportunities available at the site? Will they satisfy the couple's vision or will the couple want to leave the site to take additional pictures, which will require transportation if there is nothing of interest within walking distance.

Make sure you visit holding rooms, parking areas, entrance areas and restrooms.

Inquire about the number of events held simultaneously at the venue.

What is provided in the holding area and is it for the entire bridal party or just the couple. Is this space available before the ceremony for the bride to dress?

There are many options for venues these days and each

type of venue has its own specific set of needs and things for you, the planner to consider:

*Parks*: Are licenses required and what types of activities are covered under the license. Is alcohol allowed? If so, make sure you are aware of your area's liquor license regulations.

*Beaches*: All of the above also pertain to beaches but in addition, make sure you are aware of the time of high and low tides.   Take into account sand mites, jellyfish and other creatures.  How far away is your load-in and how much time will it take to set up?  Consider the privacy factor as well. Many beaches will not guarantee keeping onlookers away during the ceremony.  Will this be an issue for the couple?

*Private residences*: Seems like a good idea to have everything at home if the residence is large enough, but there are still quite a number of factors to consider. How much actual space do you have for guests? Is there space for a caterer to set up, cook and plate meals? Will furniture need to be removed? Will portable toilets be needed, Homeowners association rules, outdoor heating and cooling assistance...

Ready to move on? Next we look at...

## GUEST LIST:

Yes, guest list. Because up until this point your couple has been volleying around round numbers that sound good. Get them to put pencil to paper.  They will hate this and they will fight you on it. Insist and wait patiently.  If nothing else is going on while you are waiting on a guest list from them I guarantee you will get a list sooner rather than later, as they will want to move on to more fun items.

Why is this so important at such an early stage? Because it begins conversations that people often don't want to have.

Has your couple set the ground rules for their guest lists? What is the feeling on guests bringing a guest? What about co-workers? What about those relative that "have to be invited but won't show up?" Can we pause here for a moment? My philosophy is if you send an invitation expect the guest to come until they actually tell you otherwise. Your couple is inviting family and friends that love them and want to share with them and other family members. What better reason to take a trip than a wedding? *"If everyone else is going, we should too... Let's rent a van and we all can go."* All of a sudden those guests you were expecting to be a No are now a yes...

When pen is put to paper and all of these questions are answered you have a much better gauge of what the list actually looks like and can give a realistic assessment based on standard attrition.

As you go through the planning process this list will ebb and flow until you are ready to actually place an invitation order and mail those babies out.

**CHAPTER FOURTEEN**

# BUIDING YOUR TEAM

## USING INDEPENDENT CONTRACTORS:

I firmly believe that one person cannot effectively execute a wedding or event. I base this on a number of factors that many people entering into the field do not consider. Multiple locations: Perhaps the ceremony and reception are being held at two different locations. You need to have coverage at both locations to ensure they are set up to your expectation BEFORE the arrival of guests and your client and BEFORE your vendors leave. Another aspect new planners do not consider is what I call the Twenty Questions factor: Twenty different people are going to ask you twenty different questions every twenty minutes. Now understand the people asking these questions usually do not really need the answers. Overly helpful guests and family and friends are inquiring out of love, but can really usurp a lot of your time and focus, when you must stop to provide them with information that they really do not need. Having a group of people that understand the way you approach events is a great resource. They can be paid on an event by event basis. As an independent contractor you will be able to report wages for them annually and they will be able to ensure they have paid adequate income taxes.

*20 People*

*20 Questions*

*Every*

*20 Minutes*

## USING INTERNS:

The difference between an intern and an independent contractor will usually show up in the amount of experience they will bring to the table. You should be able to allow one of your independent contractors to lead an event while you are overseeing another event across town. An intern however will shadow you and learn the business through your eyes using the events you execute as hands on experience.

## SECURING VENDORS:

How you go about securing vendors may differ a little depending on where you are. It is paramount to know that before you recommend any vendor, you need to know something about them. The development of a vendor database is crucial. This is an item that needs to be maintained and updated regularly. How you choose to compile that database is a personal choice but it needs to be backed up and it needs to be accessible to everyone in your firm.

Getting to know vendors is not difficult, word of mouth referrals from others in the industry, the vendors you see repeatedly highlighted in magazines because of their innovative work, networking events will also allow you to see who is out there and what they are doing. They want to know you as much as you want to know them. Just a couple rules I would suggest following:

Send an email requesting a meeting with the vendor and follow up with a phone call of introduction. If at all possible avoid Fridays or weekends and evenings. These are the times vendors are most heavily dealing with paying clients. If you want to have a quality meeting try a mid week late morning timeslot.

Here in the Mid Atlantic area I have found that once your venues are secured turning to photography is a wise choice. There are a plethora of photographers in just about every market however the work of a photographer is the one lasting item your client will have from their wedding and there needs to be a connection with the person capturing the occasion. The more they have to choose from, the happier your client will be with their choice. Most photographers will only shoot one event per day. Once they are booked, they are booked. For these reasons, I start here.

Has the photographer you are considering ever shot at your location? Have them provide previous work at the chosen venue and get an idea of how they see the space.

Understand the difference between a photography assistant and a second shooter. A second shooter is just that; an additional person shooting images of your event and an assistant is normally there to aid the main photography, carry cameras and equipment. If possible ask to view past work of the second shooter.

Who will design your clients' album? Is a DVD of all the day's images included and are they Hi Resolution? Open the discussion regarding coverage for engagement sessions, attendance at the rehearsal and rehearsal dinner and even your engagement party. Don't forget post reception (day after) sessions and Trash the Dress sessions. Discuss timeframes. How long before proofs are available online? How long does an album layout take, once images are chosen? How long does album production take once proofs are approved? Deciding how many hours you will need a photographer will take all the factors you have already made decisions on into account.

Will the couple see each other before the ceremony? are

all activities taking place at one location? Will the couple want to go to a specific location in between the ceremony and reception? And lastly will the bride want to have Getting ready shots taken before the ceremony.

## WHAT ARE YOU LOOKING FOR?

There are questions that you ask a vendor and then there are questions that you ask a vendor *in front of a client*. Please learn the difference.

As the professional you are looking to the vendor to work in partnership with you. Would you partner with someone you know nothing about? Your client is looking to you to guide them and look out for their best interests. You are an *Advocate* for your client. You should be maintaining a database with pertinent information on your vendors. This way anyone in your office can make competent recommendations based on criteria that is provided by a client. Now I am not necessarily saying that you should work with an exclusive vendor for any service. That will only work if you are only going to work with one type of client, which you can not control. The right vendor for the right client is what you are looking to accomplish, not trying to make one vendor fit every given situation.

## CAKE BAKERS:

The only wedding cakes baked the day of a wedding are done by your Aunt Hilda. Not a professional cake baker. Can we just establish that right now. Professional cake design is a science. Accurate measurements, precise baking time and adequate cooling time are required. It takes several days to create a cake that is both beautiful and stable enough to withstand being on display at a wedding for several hours.

Understand delivery and set up fees, make sure you are clear on who will decorate the cake with live flowers, if needed, and when those flowers need to be made available.

Know the difference between flavors, fillings and icings. Are they included in the price of the cake? Does the shape of the cake impact the cost per slice? Can the baker recreate from a picture or will they provide a rendering for your client?

Discuss cake plateaus (cake stands) and anniversary tiers. Is there a fee for these services or are they complimentary?

How are cake tastings performed? This is a biggie as more and more bakers are going the route of using cupcakes for the tasting. They are now leaving the couple to mix and match flavors with fillings and icing of their own choosing. This can make for a wealth of options so be sure to keep the couple focused.

Please ensure that a box is left with the cake upon delivery. I understand it is the baker's delivery person's responsibility, but remember, *IT'S ALL your responsibility.*

VIDEOGRAPHY:

What's the difference between *Videography* and *Feature Film* coverage? Video has come a long way and many of the end products can actually take your breath away. Do not leave this as an afterthought for it is a material investment of at least a couple thousand dollars. Discuss the number of cameras needed/desired and the number of *manned* cameras needed.

What is the difference?  A manned camera will allow a person to move around while an unmanned or stationery camera will provide coverage from a fixed location.

What is the turnaround time for a fully edited video? How many copies of the video are included? Can they integrate footage from your honeymoon or rehearsal dinner or childhood photos? Are you able to choose your own background music? Is there an additional cost for adding special features like chapter breaks, slow motion etc.?

## DISC JOCKEYS:

Here lies one of the biggest make or breaks moments to a great party. The DJ. Take the time to identify professional DJ's that are familiar with performing at weddings and professional functions.  A radio/club DJ offers a different type of service.  The wedding DJ is tasked with more than merely playing music, this is your emcee for the evening and the person that must interact with the crowd and keep the party going. Club DJ's rarely have to speak formally and when transplanted at a wedding they can come across as uncomfortable, and unprofessional when they begin to speak in front of the crowd of guests.

Inquire about the ability to secure specialty music (i.e. World music, cultural selections, music created by unsigned artists etc.)

Many professional DJ's are using assistants and sound techs.  Be sure to inquire about this, it is a Win for your event.   The sound tech is essentially another set of technical arms and legs to the DJ. They can be the person correcting a problem while your event is in full flow without there being a break in the music.  It allows flow and continuity, not to mention this person will assist the DJ with load in and strike making install quick and smooth.

More and more DJ's are also offering lighting services. Depending upon the "type" of lighting they are offering and the expertise they are able to bring, this *could* be a cost saving measure for your clients, however keep in mind the old Spanish saying "*Lo barato sale caro*" which translates into "If you buy cheaply, you pay dearly." We'll speak more about lighting a little later and what makes for quality lighting.

## TRANSPORTATION:

Transportation options are extremely varied and you as a planner must do your due diligence in this area. In my opinion, you cannot have enough contacts in this category. Limousines, town cars, shuttles, coaches, vintage cars, exotic cars, trolleys, carriages, even school busses.

> "*Lo barato sale caro*" ...
>
> "If you buy cheaply, you pay dearly."

Visit and see the inventory, inquire as to whether the inventory is owned or sub-contracted. Many transportation companies will borrow vehicles from others in the business; you want to be sure they can deliver what they promise.

If you are expecting a classic understated black 10 passenger limousine and you have a shiny white 22-passenger Hummer limousine arrive, your client may not be happy with the upgrade. Confirm the minimum number of hours required (this is especially crucial during Prom season!!) and the availability of point to point transfers which are helpful to getting your client back home at the end of the evening.

## FLORISTS:

Now you have florists and you have floral designers. Understanding the difference is important. If you choose to use a florist, you may be looking at Teleflora albums of floral arrangements and choose a stock number for the arrangement that best fits your clients needs.    In some instances this will suffice. It is pretty cut and dry and you will receive exactly what you expect upon delivery.

If what you are envisioning is sitting with someone to create a look based on your space, theme, and the couple you will really need to work with a floral designer. They will take the time you will require to be innovative.  A florist will have an additional drain on resources that stem from filling delivery orders, holiday orders and funerals. Stay away from a traditional florist near Valentine's  Day and Mother's Day as they will be swamped!

Does the florist you choose have access to a wide number of wholesalers?   These are the distributors they use to procure their floral inventory. Flowers are flown in from all over the world and are ordered well in advance. How many designers are available and can you work directly with a designer to create arrangements for this event? What are the delivery and set up charges?

How many locations will they deliver to?  Keep in mind you will have personal flowers that may need to go to the bride's home or hotel, ceremony florals that need to go to a place of worship and reception arrangements going to yet a third venue.

What is the method of communication available on the day of the event (weekend?) Do they have an emergency number? Will you have the number for their driver? How many events are the capable of servicing on a weekend? How have they decorated the venue that you plan to use, in the past? Do they have images of their past work rather than stock photos?

## CATERING:

When using an in-house caterer, your leeway is limited, but by asking questions you may be amazed at the flexibility you do indeed possess.

Sample menus, can be helpful, but I often find that your providing a sample menu to the caterer instead of the opposite way, changes the conversation and you can get them talking as to how they might improve upon your suggestions.

Discuss wine pairings, organic ingredient options, service style, course options, the list is endless. Your caterer is vitally important. Don't buy into the myth that wedding food or wedding cake for that matter is terrible. Excite the senses by putting some thought and work into the menu and its presentation.

If you are considering an off premise caterer you have the luxury of shopping until you find the caterer that really meets your needs and understands what you are trying to achieve. Inquire with this type of caterer many of the logistic items that don't arise with in-house operations. Do they own their own equipment or will they be renting it and passing that cost onto the client? Can they prepare fried items onsite and ensure they are crisp? Is there a fuel charge for their trucks?

With both types of catering, never leave the question of the vegetarian option off the table; make sure that it is as appetizing as an entrée with meat.

Discuss Vegan and Kosher options. These are very strict methods of food preparation. Allergies are another area of great sensitivity. Your client will need to have at least a cursory understanding of their guests that have allergies. Asking on the RSVP card is a great way to ensure specific needs are met.

Make sure to inquire as to the ratio of wait staff to tables. Ensuring the count is high enough for your specific event is far too often the one key to a successful event that many planners overlook. It will be money well spent, should you decide the need exists, to increase the number of servers per table.

If your client has a specific taste in wines, inquire about corkage fees as an option. This will allow them to bring in their own offerings and have them served by the wait staff on hand. Does your caterer carry a liquor license and does it transfer for off premise catering? If not make sure you are versed in state laws pertaining to the serving of alcohol and when permits are required. Not to mention how, where, how much and when to apply for them.

And can we speak about Tastings???

Most people who ask me about my job inevitably ask how am I able to stay so thin when I am at tastings every day. The answer to that question is simple. IT'S A TASTING... not a five course meal with seconds.

Do not attend tastings with your client and eat as if you have just discovered food, because it is free. The tasting is to get an understanding of not only how the food tastes, but how does it work and how will it look? Will a certain hors d'oeuvres work for a woman carrying a glass of wine and a clutch purse while standing in heels? Not if it is crumbly and takes more than one bite.

How does the food look on the plate, does the plate need more color? Do the sauces work together in a duet entrée? Take notes, look at the responses from the group, ask for additional suggestions. Often times I only taste the food when I have to be a tie breaker. This is not lunch, it is business.

So whether this is planning for a wedding or another type of event all these questions need to be posed to all of these vendors.

Specific to weddings however you have:

## THE BRIDAL SALON:

Most brides have scoured magazines and websites looking at gowns and this does help to familiarize them with current styles and trends.

Very rarely does a bride take a photo of a dress from a magazine go to a salon try it on and buy it. The wedding dress experience is about more than just purchasing a dress. Brides are looking for that moment when they are treated like royalty and they find The Dress, while surrounded by family and friends. A beautiful well appointed salon with champagne and a friendly knowledgeable staff bringing dress after dress.

This is possible. But always keep in your arsenal those shops that specialize in discontinued styles, samples, and budget pricing. Design, fabric, lace and workmanship all impact the cost of a gown. A lot of work goes into gown manufacturing and the price reflects that. Purchasing a past season gown or sample will give you a quality garment at a fraction of the cost.

I suggest limiting the number of people at the very first visit. Bringing all of your client's bridesmaids, mothers, grandmothers, aunts, childhood friends, sorority sisters and the like is a method for disaster on the first visit. Take one trusted person and the bride. Your expertise should make this a successful venture. Bring a strapless bra;

many better salons will also have them available in varying sizes along with robes. You should know this before you go or inquire when you set the appointment for the bride.

Make sure everyone is on the same page with budget, and try on gowns within the budget. Try on **all** the basic gown shapes: Ball Gown, A Line, Drop Waist, Empire, Mermaid, something with and without straps and a Halter. This will allow the bride to see herself in the most flattering shape accenting her best assets and covering problem spots.

After shape of gown consider fabric: light like organza and chiffon or more substantial like satin or taffeta. What are her feelings toward lace? From there let the bride go wild with her new found information. Now she can locate a "pretty" gown with her friends and family because she has "*rules*" to follow. Keep in mind as well that many designers can lengthen trains and seamstresses can add or remove beading to suit personal tastes making the gown perfect for your bride.

VEILS:

The right veil will transform a bride and elevate her style, the wrong veil will resemble a shroud. Understanding veil length and being able to visually look at the gown and the bride to suggest the correct veil will come with time. Having a working knowledge of veil styles and lengths is a must.

You as the planner need to do some work on bustles, knowing the options available and how to pin them quickly and efficiently at the wedding. Equally this important in making a recommendation on what type of bustle should be put on the gown from the beginning. A gown in a heavy fabric is going to require something more substantial that a couple of hook and eyes to hold it together. You will need to be able to speak up and stick to your guns in this area or you will find yourself running behind a bride all night long, trying to secure an ailing bustle that refuses to stay put and interferes with the bride's ability to dance and move freely.

Be sure to inquire at the salon if alterations are included? Normally they are not and I always include a line item in the budget to cover this cost. Will the salon contact a manufacturer that they carry and have a specific sample brought in if they don't carry it so your client can try it on? Do they steam gowns? Is there a discount offered on other items if the wedding gown is purchased there (i.e. veils, bridesmaids dresses, shoes etc.)?

## ATTIRE FOR GENTLEMEN:

Tuxedos are a logical segue right here. I will impart my own personal opinions here. A tuxedo can offer a great deal of style and formality to an event, but there is a fine line between stylish and foolish. There are a lot of options available but get something that suits the body of the man wearing it. He can still have a little swerve!! I take men out ALONE. I do not need a bride telling him what to wear, HE'S a Grown Man! Allow him to work it out the same way the bride tries on fifteen dresses until she finds the one right for her!

A few tips:

- The taller you are the more buttons you can wear. A 5'7" groom wearing a tuxedo with six buttons is a clown suit. (my opinion...)

- If you must rent, remain classic. Black is timeless. Think about it this way...

  *The infamous baby blue tuxedo with the ruffle shirt was once fashionable too... You should look back at your wedding pictures 25 years from now and appear timeless. James Bond never lost it.*

  - Buy your own shirt and go for French cuffs and cufflinks. You deserve it.

  - Neckwear is a great place to add some personality. Skip the rental tie and purchase something that *coordinates* (not matches) with the event color scheme. Neck tie or Bow tie.

  - The Ascot: If you are not that guy that would whip out an ascot that you currently own and wear it to an event, then your wedding is probably not the time to try this out. Wearing an ascot takes a certain kind of swerve that owns

the selection. YOU have to wear it and not let it
WEAR YOU.

- Tip: A neck tie is meant to reach the top of a
  man's slacks. If you are trying to wear a larger
  knot have a tie made for you  to account for the
  larger knot. PLEASE stop the practice of
  shortening the tie and giving the appearance that
  you are wearing a tie made for a three year old
  child.

- The white tuxedo is not for everybody, but I tend
  not to fight folks on this one if they really want it.

- Custom made suits are always a plus though not
  always cost effective.  The better it fits, the better
  you look.

- If you are renting, opt for a chain that has
  locations nationally allowing your attendants to
  be fitted wherever they are but pick up their
  garments *locally*  so as not to arrive with a
  wrinkled suit or have it lost on a plane causing
  additional fees.

- White tie is the **most** formal option available.

- Black tie is formal and just as an FYI **Black  tie  is
  not  optional**, it either is or it isn't. If you desire a
  formal event, deem it Black Tie.  By stating this
  you are not putting a gun to anyone's head and
  making them rent a tuxedo, what you are doing
  however, is putting them on notice that they will
  be in a formal environment. Take a stand.

**CHAPTER FIFTEEN**

# CREATING THE EXPERIENCE

The players are in place, the team has been formed. You have an infrastructure created now is the time to add the elements. How you add them is as important as what elements you add.

Yes, we are finally there.

# Design.

Design has been defined as "*An adaptation of means to a preconceived end. To plan and fashion artistically or skillfully. To form or conceive in the mind, contrive or plan. To assign in thought or intention to intend for one's definite purpose.*"

Event design is an artistic ability to visualize and create a memorable experience.

In perusing the above definitions there is one word which is glaringly absent from each of them. That word is Copy.

This is a bit of a personal pet peeve for me, (I know I have a lot of pet peeves...) why would one want to be called a designer if all that is done has been created by someone else?

Answer: Because, no one wants to be called a copier or an imitator. We all want to be unique and original but often lack the creative genesis or the work ethic to spur that creative genesis. Now that we have gotten that out into the open let us work on changing it.

## COLOR:

Understanding color. Warms and cools, Pastel and Jewel tones... We see color everywhere, makeup, clothing, hair color, nail color. Granted not everyone has great looking makeup, clothing, hair or nails but we do interact with color all of the time.

Warm colors are hues at the Red-Yellow end of the color spectrum. They are based on yellows, oranges, browns, yellowish greens, orangy reds, and the like.

Cool colors are based on blues, greens, pinks, purples, blue-greens, magentas, and blue-based reds. Once you have a basic understanding, you can then differentiate between a "warm pink" and a "cool pink". A warm pink is a peachy pink. A cool pink would be a purplish pink. A warm green would be a yellowish green. A cool green would be more blue.

This is a key point in creating color palettes. Very often we ask the client "what are your colors" and the response is two contrasting or coordinating colors. Pink and Purple. This is the foundation for a very flat look. It will be "matchy-matchy", not what we are looking for. To develop warmth, depth and texture you need to be able to integrate a palette of colors. A varying shade of hues that progress from a lighter shade to a darker shade. This is interesting to the eye.

Even when you look at nature you see that not every rose on a bush is exactly the same as every other rose. Some are smaller or larger, there are tinges of color on certain petals while not on others.

Once you can effectively work with color, have the ability to interchange it and know what is missing to fill a void using both color and texture. You are on your way to creating majesty.

## INSPIRATION:

Inspiration, I believe, is where many get hung up and fall prey to Imitation. You can be inspired by something and have that item or image spark an idea in your head. The genesis can *remind* you of something or perhaps it holds the solution on how to make something operate or be the remedy for another part of a current idea to become feasible in its construction or execution.

That is inspiration. I recently came across the photograph below of a couple standing at a doorway entrance and above them is an enormous starburst chandelier. It is a gorgeous picture with exaggerated scale.

But what did I see? What were my immediate thoughts? I thought that this chandelier would be the perfect centerpiece. I took the picture to a florist and we sat down together for several hours going over how we could design a centerpiece in homage to this chandelier. What materials should be used and how do we capture the brilliance of the piece? Should it be metal? Glass? Plexiglass? What kinds of flowers would work, how many flowers would it take to cover it, but still allow the piece to shine through and not look like a flower covered frame? How do we price it? After many drawings and sketches the florist took our ideas to a metal fabricator and had the frame designed. Once the frame was designed we worked at covering the frame with various types of flowers, we added flowers, removed flowers, changed varieties of flowers, added crystals, wrapped crystals, dangled crystals draped crystals from the structure. Was it too tall; was it in proportion to itself? To the table? The questions went on and on.... We finally got there, only to start an entirely different debate, which was the table... What else goes on the table, what kind of linen? Textured or just sheen? Should the linen be in a bold color or a neutral? If the linen is <blank> should we change the color of the all of the flowers we just decided upon to adorn the centerpiece? Stemware, flatware, china, satellite flowers...

What about lighting? Should the lighting come from the centerpiece itself as in a chandelier, should it be pinspot from above? Are the candles on the table enough to illuminate?

It took several hours on several days, but we got it. He loved, I loved it, the client loved it, and her guests were awe struck. This is the design process.

We did not have a formula, our only guideline was the objective given by the couple. What we did have was a working knowledge of all the elements needed to create a WOW! We did not know we had it until we actually got there and we had woven our way through many trials and errors.

The ability and willingness to do this over and over is the make of a designer.

Sometimes inspiration comes from the need to solve a challenge or work around an existing impediment.

We had a client of Asian descent that wanted to pay homage to her heritage and properly introduce her Texan born and bred husband and his family into her family's world. The reception took place at a very traditional Chinese restaurant. Overly ornate and designed in the mid 80's with teal, red and gold. The ceilings were inlaid with trays of different shapes and sizes, nothing about the space had symmetry. The walls were heavily adorned with large golden dragons and phoenixes and other symbols. In a word the scene was trite and expected.

The bride, however, was the picture of high fashion and chicness. She absolutely hated the space. But the space was able to accommodate her more than 300 guests and to its credit, had the best authentic cuisine in the metropolitan area. The meal was to be thirteen courses served family style on a spinning Lazy Susan at every table.

My challenge: To transform the space into a chic interpretation of Asian culture and create a statement centerpiece that would work on a table with a centralized Lazy Susan while providing guests easy access to their family style meal.

The solution: Work with, not against the issues in the room. We brought in hundreds of yards of sheer fabric and worked with the curves of each of the tray ceilings, draping fabric ceiling to floor. The fabric created smaller intimate vignettes consisting of a small number of tables clustered together. The fabric was then pulled back drapery style and held with ornate pullbacks. The walls were a bright red and we used a red palette bring in deeper reds and burgundies. The abundance of the fabric actually turned the walls into the accent for the room, rather than the primary color. The draped fabric covered the teal trey ceilings taking that obstacle out of play.

The result was a space so transformed that the owners of the restaurant who had been hosting events in this space for more than 20 years, were awestruck. They had never imagined their space looking like anything other than a restaurant.

That only rectified one of our challenges though. We still had to figure out what was going to adorn the tables? Now that we had all of this wonderful fabric hanging from the ceiling it eliminated the option of using suspended arrangements, as I am sure each of you immediately considered.

So back to the drawing board we went and of course that drawing board lead us to partner up with a spectacular floral designer. We actually posed the challenge to three different designers and only one of them came back with a 100% viable option. As I mentioned earlier, one tried and true design rule to adhere to when trying to adhere to a budget is to work with your existing circumstance not against it. While we did that with the space and the ceilings and the walls, this philosophy almost escaped us when it came to our tables. We couldn't use the ceiling as that was taken and we couldn't use the tabletop as that was occupied by a 36" Lazy Susan, so all that appeared to be left was the space in between. Genius!!

The designer fabricated a metal base to fit over the Lazy Susan exactly. It had a round 36" metal base that sat flush on the surface of the Lazy Susan and still allowed the food dishes to be placed upon it with any encumbrance. It also allowed the Lazy Susan to spin so that guests could still share all of the courses as they were served.

Spouting from the flat base was a 36" tall spire with a 9" plate on top. The smaller base allowed florals to be placed atop the larger base without coming in contact with guests or the table.

The designer then created a lush arrangement of deep red and burgundy Mokara orchids that, in essence, became large floral umbrellas over each table.

The magic began as guests were served their courses and began to spin the Lazy Susan's causing the florals to spin. Each table moved independent of the others but the entire room was in motion. Glorious!!!

We added a bit of pinspot lighting, lowered the overhead lighting and Voila! Magic.

# EPILOGUE

And so a dent has been made in the process. Proverbs 16:3 (NIV) states:

*"Commit to the Lord whatever you do and He will establish your plans."*

Understand that this indeed is a process and it will take time for global change to manifest. You must remain intentional. You will need commitment and patience for this journey but it will prove worth your effort. You will still be dealing with people who are set in their ways and resistant to change. There will still be people who want to be in charge and possibly resent your ability to manage projects on this level.

That is not where our focus is to be set. It is not about us or those that want to stand in objection, it is about Christ and those that have a need and desire to get to him and are seeking a path.

Proverbs 16:9 (NIV) goes on to state:

*"In their hearts humans plan their course. But the Lord establishes their steps."*

This is a powerful word when looked at both from the standpoint of we, who feel a desire to work for the Lord and have followed a path that leads us to where we are today and as well from the standpoint of those whose lives God has directed to us at this moment in time. Those lives who have not yet reached the place we find ourselves in Him but He still saw fit to use us as He orders their steps in the right direction.

Every ministry is different in the way they may approach the operations portion of their experience and as long as it is comprehensive, inclusive and produces results then you are in a good place.

My goal for writing this book was to say on the record what I have heard reiterated by "church going" folk for years; "We've Got To Do Better." And we do. But the key is we ALL have to do better. This is not to finger point at any one area, if the mark is being missed, we've all missed it.

The objective of the church is to save souls. There is more to what we do than merely minister to those that already believe. There is a balance that has to be maintained in order to do both. We do not like to talk about how many people we may have turned off on any given day for any given reason. There is more to this than the blatant outright rudeness which we are quick to point out, but who gives thought to how some of our actions may be much more subtle and throw off the preacher and knock him off his game?

Many churches are growing exponentially and find themselves working to stay ahead of the curve. When your church is thriving and members are hungry they create a buzz that non members pick up on and want to be aligned beside.

A 100 member church that adds two members each Sunday will grow by 100% in just one year. But what are they doing to attract two new members a week while maintaining and engaging the original 100 that are currently members?

While I do believe it is important to keep a global vision you can only implement one step at a time with the understanding that Yes, you will have misses but you will also hit a few out of the ball park. Perfection is neither attainable nor sustainable but giving a 100% effort can be accomplished each and every day.

My hope and goal is that we cease just accepting that things are just the way that they are and we give the Kingdom of God the effort that it deserves. I think back to my own interpretation of the Great Commission and how I personally have been gifted to operate my thoughts about this book and have this arm of ministry grow.

*Jesus, undeterred, went right ahead and gave his charge: "God authorized and commanded me to commission you: Go out and train everyone you meet, far and near, in this way of life, marking them by baptism in the threefold name: Father, Son, and Holy Spirit. Then instruct them in the practice of all I have commanded you. I'll be with you as you do this, day after day after day, right up to the end of the age."*

The Message

My calling does not mandate that I be in the forefront and I find that I am truly effective when I am unleashed behind the scenes. I get a sense of fulfillment when I see a small cue work that wasn't there before because I can appreciate the difference it has made on the event as a whole. I celebrate every person that walks the aisle at the end of a service or ministry event because something went right that could have gone wrong. Jonathan Nelson penned it appropriately in the words of his song *"It could have been another way."* God uses me in this way and I have to believe there are others who are like minded and will embrace the work we still have to accomplish.

# GLOSSARY

**A/V:** Acronym that stands for Audio/Visual, relating to equipment for hearing or sight.

**Acolyte:** A person who assists in the worship service. Normally the acolyte serves by lighting and extinguishing the candles on the communion or altar table. At the discretion of the pastor, the acolyte may also assist in other portions of the worship service. It is the custom in most churches for the acolytes to be young persons, giving them an early opportunity to be participants in the service. Adults, however, also may serve as acolytes.

**Actual Cost:** Costs that have been derived from historical data or actual quotes; not estimates or budgeted costs.

**Adjutant:** An assistant trained to the specific needs of the person to whom they are assigned.

**Agent:** A certified representative who has the proper credentials from the person they are representing.

**Aisle:** A walkway specifically created for audience movement through an exposition, exhibit or function.

**Altar:** The altar is the table clergy use for Communion.

**Auxilary Services:** Services that are contracted in support of a function.

**Back-light:** A light source set behind a translucent material.

**Banquet Event Order:** Also know as a "BEO." A guideline containing event details for the Event Managers on site on the day of an event.

**Baptistry:** In churches that administer baptism by

immersion, the baptistry is a  pool that is located in the church for this purpose.

**Book:** To make a reservation for a specific room, space or service at a particular time with payment agreed upon.

**Breakeven Point:** The  quantity to be reached in order to receive a discount based on volume.

**Budget**: A fundamental tool for an event director to predict with reasonable accuracy whether the event will result in a profit, a loss or will break-even .

**Butlered Service:** Service style where servers walk amongst guests passing hors d'oeuvres on trays.

**Cancellation Policy:** Document that states the actions that can and will be taken in the event of a cancellation due to certain circumstances.

**Charger**: A plate that separates the eating plate from the table and is used for decoration. Technically used to protect a table from a hot plate.

**Charter:** Exclusive rental, hire or lease for temporary use.

**Cherry Picker:** Large equipment used to lift people to a given height.

**Chevron Seating:** Seating  design where the room is set with tables and/or chairs in a V.

**Chiavari Chair**: Decorative commercial wood,  resin, or metal stackable ballroom chair that come in all colors. They come with optional padded or cloth seats and are known for their resemblance to bamboo.

**Chuppah:** <also Huppah> A Hebrew word that describes a canopy traditionally used in Jewish weddings. It consists of a cloth or fabric supported over four poles which can be carried to the wedding ceremony.

**Classroom Seating:** Seating design where the room is set with rows facing the front of the room and each person has their own writing table.

**Clean Bill of Lading:** A receipt issued to a carrier indicating that the transported merchandise was received in apparent good condition.

**Color Wash**: A colored lighting used to create ambiance in a space.

**Communion:** The sacrament often called the Lord's Supper.

**Concierge:** Staff member who handles specific requests for guests or visitors.

**Conference Seating:** Seating design arrangement where the room is set with chairs that are placed around all sides of a table.

**Confirmation:** Official verification of a reservation that outlines the initial plans for the use a product or service that may also serve as the contract.

**Congregation** - broadly understood as those present at a religious service. Technically baptized members of a Christian community.

**Consignee:** The person or agent to whom goods are shipped.

**Consignment:** An arrangement between the person or consignor who exports the merchandise and the person or consignee who receives the merchandise that will then be sold, giving the consignee a commission and the consignor the net proceeds of the merchandise.

**Consignor:** A person or agent who sends goods to the consignee.

**Contract**: A legal document between two parties. This document is usually accompanied by a money deposit and highlights very specific agreements of both parties.

**Contractor:** A paid professional individual or company that provides services or materials.

**Covenant:** The entering into and committing oneself to a continuing relationship.

**Crisis Management:** Actions taken by an organization in response to unexpected events or situations that could have potentially negative effects.

**D/B/A:** Acronym that stands for Doing Business As, often used for companies using different names for different areas of the business.

**D.O.T.:** Acronym for Department of Transportation.

**D/T Labor:** Refers to Double Time Labor or any work performed on overtime that is charged at twice the published rate.

**Dais:** A raised platform where guest speakers, honored guests or expert panels are seated.

**Deacon:** An ordained clergyperson who is called to serve all people and to equip and lead the laity in ministries of compassion, justice and service in the world. A deacon has the authority to teach and proclaim God's Word, to lead in worship, to assist elders in the administration of the sacraments of Holy Baptism and Holy Communion.

**Deaconess:** A laywoman who, commissioned by a bishop to share faith in Jesus Christ through ministries of love, justice and service.

**Dead Time:** Also known as down time, a period of time when, due to factors beyond their control, workers are unable to perform their duties.

**Deliverable**: A tangible or intangible object produced as a result of the project that is intended to be delivered to a customer.

**Denomination:** The body of persons or the organization formed around a particular set of religious beliefs or structure or type of government.

**Discipleship:** The active living of the individual Christian in accordance with the teachings of Jesus Christ. Discipleship involves a ministry of outreaching love and witness to others concerning Christ and God's grace. Discipleship also calls the Christian to ministries of servanthood and service to the world to the glory of God and for human fulfillment.

**Dismantle:** The tearing down or taking apart of an exhibit after an event is over.

**Elevations:** Scaled drawings of an exhibit that depict front and side views.

**Fabrication:** The construction or creation of an exhibit.

**Faith Based**: term coined in the 1970's to describe any organization or plan based on religious beliefs, specifically Christian belief.

**Final Guarantee** - The final expected number of guests.

**Floor Plan:** A scaled drawing or map showing the arrangement of rooms, as well as the size and locations of the exhibit spaces.

**Four Hour Call:** Union labor must be paid for a minimum work period of four hours.

**Generator**: A supply of energy that converts one type of energy to another. Generators prevent blackouts from the overuse of a power.

**Gobo**: Lighting projected onto a stencil to create a logo or design on a wall or surface. Ex., companies can request that their logo or company name be embossed on the wall.

**Gospel:** From the Latin *evangelium*, meaning good tale or good news. Gospel has a number of distinct meanings. It refers to the Good News concerning Christ, the Kingdom of God, and salvation. It also refers to the teachings of Jesus and the apostles. The word is used in connection with the first four books of the New Testament.

**Head Count:** Number of people attending an event.

**Hierarchy**: An arrangement of items in which the items are represented as being "above," "below," or "at the same level as" one another.

**Honorarium**: A payment given to a professional person for services for which fees are not legally or traditionally required.

**Hors D'oeuvres:** Hot and/or cold finger foods served at a reception.

**Independent Contractor:** A contractor hired to perform services independently of your firm while following your plans.

**Introit**: A hymn or song for an entrance.

**Invocation:** A prayer asking for a special sense of God's presence and guidance. The invocation is offered at an early point in a service of worship or at the beginning of a meeting or other event.

**Keynote:** Opening remarks of a meeting that set tone of the event and motivate attendees.

**Keynote Speaker:** One who presents the issues of primary interest to a group of people.

**Lavaliere Microphone:** A small microphone that is clipped onto clothing to allow the speaker to move.

**Linen:**Cloth used on eating tables and to decorate the tables in line with the rest of the décor of the room.

**Loading Dock:** An area where freight is received and shipped.

**Logistics**: The time-related positioning of resources

**Media  or ( Press) Kit:** A package of materials put together for the media, usually contained in a folder, in which news releases, product announcements and other materials intended for the media are distributed.

**Press (or Media) Release:** Description of a newsworthy occurrence written in journalistic or unbiased style and mailed to the news media. A press release is usually intended to promote an event or further the reputation of a facility.

**Mission:** A short written statement of purpose.

**Narthex:**The main foyer or entry way of the church.

**New Testament:** The twenty-seven books accepted by Christians as authoritative or canonical concerning the life of Christ and the experience of the early Christian church.

**Old Testament:** The thirty-nine books of the pre-Christian era considered authoritative and canonical by most Protestant churches.

**Ordination:** The act of conferring ministerial orders, presided over by a bishop.

**Pin Spot:** Spot lights directed at something specific.

**Pipe and Drape:** Tubing rails (pipe) that are covered with draped fabric (drape) To create backdrops  or booths.

**Podium:** A small raised platform at which a presenter may stand.

**Press (or Media) Kit:** A package of materials put together for the media, usually contained in a folder, in which news releases, product announcements and other materials intended for the media are distributed.

**Press (or Media) Release:** Description of a newsworthy occurrence written in journalistic or unbiased style and mailed to the news media. A press release is usually intended to promote an event or further the reputation of a facility.

**Psalmist:** A writer or composer of psalms.  A singer.

**Publicity:** Information that attracts attention to a company, product, person, or event.

**Pulpit:** Area by clergy to read the gospel and preach the sermon.

**RACI:** Responsibility Assignment Matrix describes the participation by various roles in completing tasks or deliverables for a project or business process.

**RFP:** Acronym that stands for Request for Proposal Process. A document issued to potential bidders that outlines what products and services an organization requires, leaving specific solutions up to the supplier to suggest.

**Recovery:** The restoration of something lost or taken away.

**Resources:** Any physical or virtual entity of limited availability that needs to be consumed in order to obtain a benefit.

**Run Sheet:** A list of procedures or events organized in temporal sequence given to members of the camera and audio crew, as well as members of the stage crew, to use as a visual reference for cues throughout an event.

**Sacrament:**Something consecrated or holy.

**Sacristy:**The room or closet in which communion equipment, linen, and supplies are kept.

**Scope**: The range of one's perceptions, thoughts, or actions. The breadth or opportunity to function.

**Serpentine Table**: Curved banquet tables which can be linked together to create unusually creative table designs.

**Skirting:** Decorative fabric placed around a table or riser to conceal the area underneath.

**Sponsorship**: A business relationship between a provider of funds, resources or services and an event or organization which offers in return association that may be used for commercial advantage in return for the sponsorship investment.

**Standard Operating Procedure (SOP):** Detailed, written instructions to achieve uniformity of the performance of a specific function.

**Step Repeat:** Backdrop area on a red carpet where each person  must stop to give an interview or take a picture. It also helps the process stay organized and move smoothly.

**Up Lighting:** Par Can lighting placed on the floor so the light is directed upwards.

**Valet**: A company or persons hired to park and retrieve cars during an event for a  fee.

**Vestments:** Items of clothing, such as robes, gowns, or other special garments and stoles worn by ministers and lay persons while conducting worship services.

**Vigil:** A service or period of prayers and devotions usually held on the night before or in the early morning of important religious days or festivals. On occasion, special vigils are organized around a specific concern or issue in a local church. The word *vigil* comes from the Latin *vigilia*, meaning to watch.

**Vision**: A vivid conscious perception in the absence of a stimulus for the direction of one's organization.

**Volunteer**: People working on behalf of others without being motivated by financial or material gain.

.

# RESOURCES

Harvey Mackay, author of the New York Times #1 bestseller "*Swim With The Sharks Without Being Eaten Alive.*" *Ballantine Books New York 1988*

Hodges, Herb. 2001 *Tally Ho The Fox! (The Foundation for Building World-Visionary, World-Impacting, Reproducing Disciples)* Germantown:Spiritual Life Ministries.

Anyabwile, Thabiti. (October 11, 2010). Are Your Church Members Under-Employed?. In *The Gospel Coalition.* Retrieved October 27, 2010, from http:// t h e g o s p e l c o a l i t i o n . o r g / b l o g s / thabitianyabwile/2010/10/11/are-your-church-members -under-employed/.

Scripture quotations taken from the Amplified® Bible, Copyright © 1954, 1958, 1962, 1964, 1965, 1987 by The Lockman Foundation
Used by permission." (www.Lockman.org)

THE HOLY BIBLE, NEW INTERNATIONAL VERSION®, NIV® Copyright © 1973, 1978, 1984, 2010 by Biblica, Inc.™ Used by permission. All rights reserved worldwide.

Scripture taken from *The Message.* Copyright ◆ 1993, 1994, 1995, 1996, 2000, 2001, 2002. Used by permission of NavPress Publishing Group.

Vicky Johnson is a phenomenally dynamic personality and speaker with a diverse sphere of influence. She is owner and creative director of *holy matrimony*, a social event planning firm specializing in large scale weddings founded in 2001. The firm, with its primary offices located in Washington, DC, produces extraordinary events both nationally and internationally. The firm and Mrs. Johnson have been featured in local, regional and national publications including Redbook, Essence, Brides Noir, The Washington Post, The Baltimore Sun, The Knot, The Hill, Express and many others. She is a featured planner on Style Network's hit television show *Whose Wedding Is It Anyway?* Her reputation for logistically flawless events and snarky sense of humor that, has her firm requested by society's finest and has taken her team across the country and world.

In September, 2008 she co-launched, Haute Minded Events (HME) (www.eventsbyhm.com) a boutique firm producing non-wedding related events. Mrs. Johnson is also the creator of the widely popular and award winning wedding blog DC Nearlyweds (www.dcnearlyweds.com). The blog has received nationwide acclaim for its informative and witty content.

Named Entrepreneur of the Year in 2003 for the astounding strides her firm made in the special events industry. Mrs. Johnson has received numerous accolades and recognition since. She is a requested speaker and presenter for the International Special Event Society (ISES), Association of Bridal Consultants (ABC), and Association of Wedding Professionals (AWP). She has been featured on CNN's *American Morning* as an industry professional and served as a moderator annually for *Wedding Week* sponsored by The Washington Post. She is also the past contributing style editor for the nationally distributed *Brides Noir* magazine.

Mrs. Johnson serves as an adjunct professor instructing and certifying students in wedding and event planning at the college level. Her firm has been named to the Grace Ormonde Wedding Style's Platinum List citing excellence in her field on a national level. Most recently, she was named 2010 Bride's Choice by Weddingwire.com

The latest endeavor of this powerhouse personality is born from the personal side of her life. Having spent more than a decade actively serving in ministry, Mrs. Johnson saw an opportunity within the faith-based community. Her internal drive to serve this population has led to a dedicated focus on ministry event management; the improvement of any worship experience through the execution of flawless ministry. Divine Logistics (www.divinelogistics.org) is changing lives by improving the execution of various aspects of the ministry experience.

A believer in giving back Mrs. Johnson is an active volunteer and oversees the wedding ministry team and all weddings performed at the 7,000+ member New Psalmist Baptist Church in Baltimore, MD. While career and ministry command a large pool of time and attention, they fall second to marriage and family. Vicky is blessed to share this journey with husband John; together they parent a wonderful diversely talented set of children.

www.ingramcontent.com/pod-product-compliance
Lightning Source LLC
LaVergne TN
LVHW011230080426
835509LV00005B/416